NATURAL THEOLOGY;
OR,
RATIONAL THEISM
BY MILTON VALENTINE, D.D., LL.D.
EX-PRESIDENT OF PENNSYLVANIA COLLEGE, AND PROFESSOR OF THEOLOGY IN THE LUTHERAN THEOLOGICAL SEMINARY, GETTYSBURG, PA.

www.JustandSinner.com

NATURAL THEOLOGY BY MILTON VALENTINE

Copyright 2015 Just and Sinner. All rights reserved. The original text is in the public domain, but regarding this updated edition, besides brief quotations, none of this book shall be reproduced without permission.
Permission inquiries may be sent to JustandSinner@yahoo.com

Just & Sinner
425 East Lincoln Ave.
Watseka, IL 60970

www.JustandSinner.com

ISBN 10: 0692261591
ISBN 13: 978-0692261590

Original Publishing Info:
CHICAGO
JOHN C. BUCKBEE & CO., PUBLISHERS
122 & 124 WABASH AVENUECOPYRIGHT, 1885,
BY S. C. GRIGGS AND COMPANY

PREFACE

THIS volume presents the substance of lectures on the subject, given to students in the author's recent relation as President of Pennsylvania College. He was led to this method of instruction by the absence of any suitable text-book covering the various forms of the theistic evidences. Though the matter is here somewhat rearranged and reshaped, the general discussion has been determined by the needs of the College class room and the purpose of furnishing a reasoned and correct view of the truth on this incomparably important subject. The aim of the book, therefore, is, not to offer any new or original view of the theistic question, but to bring together the various approved evidences and furnish a compendious statement of them as they now stand in the best accredited thought and knowledge of our times. It is didactic, rather than polemical. The difficulty of the undertaking has been fully appreciated. No subject could be named, the discussion of which would lead through such a mass of conflicting metaphysics or traverse more varied and antagonistic speculation. The scientific theories and hypotheses of the recent years have greatly tended to make the basis of theism the focal point of the thought of the age. Though adverse speculation, it is believed, has not overthrown any of the old evidences in Natural Theology, it has yet made desirable such changes as shall harmonize the statement of them with the advanced knowledge now possessed. Such adjustive modification has been here attempted, as far as the necessary brevity of presentation has allowed. In consideration of the general purpose of the discussion, the author has felt at liberty to draw freely from the immense amount of literature that has been accumulated about the subject. He has at the same time endeavored to make proper acknowledgments. Though it is vain to imagine that the statement of the evidences here given will satisfy all, it is, nevertheless, hoped that its publication, in response to the frequently expressed wish of former pupils, will in some humble measure serve the great cause of truth, in supplying to students and other intelligent readers a brief view of the theistic evidences as considered apart from special revelation.

Gettysburg, Pa., June 1, 1885.

CONTENTS
INTRODUCTION...9

PART I
EVIDENCES OF THE DIVINE EXISTENCE...25

CHAPTER I
PRESUMPTIVE EVIDENCE...29
CHAPTER II
THE ONTOLOGICAL EVIDENCE...43
CHAPTER III
THE COSMOLOGICAL EVIDENCE...55
CHAPTER IV
THE TELEOLOGICAL EVIDENCE...67
CHAPTER V
THE MORAL EVIDENCE...169

PART II
THE CHARACTER OF GOD—HIS RELATIONS TO THE UNIVERSE...183

CHAPTER I
THE ATTRIBUTES OF THE DEITY...183
CHAPTER II
THE RELATION OF GOD TO THE UNIVERSE...207

Natural Theology

INTRODUCTION

I. DEFINITION AND GENERAL VIEW OF THE SUBJECT

1. NATURAL THEOLOGY treats of the *existence* and *character* of God, as these may be known from reason and nature. It investigates the evidences of His being, and seeks to determine His attributes and relation to the world. The conclusions reached through this investigation, and established as valid on just principles of evidence, form what may be accepted as Rational Theism, or the doctrine of God as ascertainable apart from supernatural revelation.

2. The fundamental idea upon which Natural Theology proceeds is that, if there be a God as the Creator or First Cause of the universe, His existence and character may and must be found impressed upon it and discoverable from it. To some degree, at least, the author of a work is necessarily revealed in the work he has done. With respect to simply human affairs this principle holds fully. In every product of thought and skill we read the existence and mind of the producer. From the rudest mechanism to the highest and most complex products of invention and the fine arts, from the roughly shaped arrowhead of savagery to the steam-engine or chronometer of science, the thing made contains and reflects the thought and purpose of the maker. The idea is fixed and legible in the product. Whatever a man in the creative energy of his will, under the guidance of his intelligence, does in the world, not only bears witness to his existence, but expresses his mind, skill, and character. The works of men reveal them even more surely than their words.

This principle has a twofold application in the investigations of Natural Theology. It is applied, *first*, with respect to the world of *mind*, or conscious human intelligence. If man is a creature of God, if his existence and nature have been given him by a Supreme First Cause, it is not only reasonable to expect, but absurd to doubt, that there is to be found in his mind some impress or reflection of His being, some mark of the workman on his work. It is fair to suppose that the human soul, or the rational nature of man, would mirror, possibly even to the soul's own consciousness, the existence of its author. To say the least, it is fair to raise the question whether this may not be so, and to settle it by its appropriate evidences. The principle is applicable, *secondly*, with respect to the *material universe*. This, not only as a whole, but in all its parts and particulars, is justly viewed as entitled to bear testimony when the question of the being and character of a Maker is investigated. Not only according to the common understanding of men, but according to the fundamental conception and basis of science, the material cosmos holds and presents in its constitution and order some records of its origin and history, legible to the reason of those who honestly study it. If anyone should allege that this is only an assumption, incapable of absolute proof, it is enough to recall the fact that it is the necessary postulate upon which all the great structures of scientific explanation of the universe are founded and built. Should it be said, as it often is, that nature conceals rather than reveals God, forming a veil behind which He is hidden as the action of physical causes goes ceaselessly on, it is freely admitted that the eye of sense cannot behold Him. But the vision of reason, interpreting these physical causes, can penetrate the veil and see the reality and glory of the Power that operates through them.

3. Natural Theology proceeds also upon the legitimacy and reliability of the so-called *intuitional, a priori*, or *necessary truths*, and of the *laws of logical thought*. It accepts as trustworthy, and as standing for objective reality, the ideas of Space, Time, Being and Relations, Substance and Attribute, and the Law of Causation. In doing so, there is no necessity of settling the dispute among philosophers as to the precise way in which they originate. For both intuitionalists and their opponents recognize that they are

essential and fundamental in human thought, incapable of being shown to be invalid or misleading, and impossible to be denied without repudiating and overthrowing the foundations of science and knowledge. Though there is no good ground to doubt the substantial correctness of the view which explains these primary truths as "intuitions" of the reason, necessarily developed in connection with and on occasion of the action of the sense-perceptions and consciousness, we need not rest their validity upon any particular explanation of their origin or any special way of designating them. It is enough to know that their authority is invincible in the practical thinking and reasoning of the race, and that science or philosophy cannot impeach them without suicide. For they are necessarily assumed in all inductive and deductive reasoning, in all the research and the essential processes through which conclusions are everywhere established. Without them logic loses all its foundation principles, and moves in air. The arguments framed to overthrow them are themselves overthrown, making plain the impossibility of refuting their ruling authority.

4. Natural Theology is a *science*. The investigation is conducted upon the accepted principles of scientific procedure. The method is that of exact observation of the realities of the mental and physical worlds, and a careful and logical interpretation of their indications under the application of the first principles and laws of thought. Nothing is to be claimed as established that is not sustained by the facts and the necessary demands of reason.

5. The relation of Natural to Christian Theology is that of part to the whole. Belief in the existence of God is presupposed in our acceptance of a revelation. Natural Theology, therefore, lies at the basis of Revealed Theology, proving the existence of a Supreme Being to reveal Himself. Revealed Theology accepts all that may be discovered and proved concerning God and His attributes from data in nature and consciousness, but adds immensely to this knowledge, especially in disclosing the scheme of grace and redemption through Jesus Christ.

6. The beginnings of effort to construct a Natural Theology appear very early. In estimating its beginning, however, we must

Natural Theology

leave out of view all the ages in which men believed in the existence of God or of some supreme power without attempts to establish it by systematic or logical proof. Natural Theology must be distinguished from natural religion, the latter appearing long before the truths it implies were regularly and distinctly formulated. Moreover, the Hebrew people, forming a circle illuminated by special revelation, must be excluded from view in this connection. Their religion was a revealed religion, and they constructed no Natural Theology. But the most ancient literatures of other nations present many of the truths of Natural Theology in more or less systematized form. The *Vedas* of the Hindus, the *Zend-Avesta* of the Persians, the *Book of the Dead* and other writings of the ancient Egyptians, contain illustrations of the earliest known efforts of the human mind toward a knowledge of God. Whatever theistic truth and faith are found among the Greeks and Romans must be counted as derived from reason and nature. Socrates and Plato, especially, among the Greeks, and Cicero and Seneca among the Romans, made earnest, and to some degree successful efforts to give rational account of men's spontaneous faith in the divine existence, and their necessary conception of His character. In all ages of the Christian Church theologians have claimed that the works of nature exhibit the power, wisdom, and goodness of their Author, and that revelation assumes this fact. To construct the knowledge thus attainable into a definite system, however, seems not, for a long time, to have awakened any marked effort. The *Theologia Naturalis sive Liber Creaturarum* of the Spanish physician, Raymond de Sabunde, teacher in the University of Toulouse in the early part of the fifteenth century, is said to have been the first work that, on the assumption that two books have been given men, one of nature and the other of revelation, confined itself to a theological interpretation of the former. Faustus Socinus, however, maintained that a Natural Theology was impossible, as no knowledge of God was attainable except from the Scriptures. In this he has had but a feeble following. During the seventeenth century, Natural Theology rose in increasing prominence, and flourished in a sort of golden age in the eighteenth. Deistical writers sought to exalt it at the expense of Christianity, representing it as the real truth, to which the Scriptures added nothing of value. They looked on Christianity as simply a "republication of natural religion." But both these extreme views, the deistical exaggerations of nature and reason on the one hand, and the denial of the possibility of Natural Theology on the other, have failed to secure or hold the confidence of well-balanced thinkers. The numerous able works which followed in the eighteenth century and since, of Clarke, Newton, Derham, Neuwentyt, Paley, and the *Bridgewater Treatises* by Chalmers, Whewell, Kidd, Roget, Buckland, and Sir Charles Bell, Lord Brougham's *Discourse on Natural Theology*, the *Burnett Prize Essays* by Thompson and Tulloch, Cooke's *Religion and Chemistry*, McCosh's *Typical Forms*, Chadbourne's *Natural Theology*, Cocker's *Theistic Conception of the World*, Flint's *Theism and Anti-Theistical Theories*, Borden P. Bowne's *Studies in Theism*, Diman's *Theistic Argument as Affected by Recent Theories*, Janet's *Final Causes* Dr. S. Harris' *Philosophical Basis of Theism*, and an immense number of review articles continually appearing, have given the subject great wealth of discussion. They have abundantly shown that while the Bible is to a large extent a republication of theistic truths and spiritual laws discernible by reason from nature and the conscience, and has, in the doctrines of redemption, given the materials of a distinctively revealed theology, there are, nevertheless, abundant sources, and a clear place, for a reliable Natural Theology, and that this is necessary as laying the deep foundations for the Christian system.

7. The importance of Natural Theology becomes evident from its relation to all the great questions and interests of life.

(1) To *religion*. If religion is to vindicate its reasonableness and right to a place in human life, it must rest on an assured knowledge of the object of worship. This is true whether it be the Christian religion or any other. Christianity is a large phenomenon in the world. Other religions, also, all rest on belief in God. Unless the question of the existence and character of God be answered, and answered so as to satisfy the reason of mankind, religion must lose its very foundation truths and die out from among men. Religion cannot stand if belief in God cannot be sustained and justified in reason.

(2) To *morality* it is hardly less essential. If experience teaches anything plainly, it is that there is no effectual dynamic for a pure, reliable, healthy morality apart from belief in the existence of God and a conviction of responsibility to Him as a holy and righteous governor. To build up a sentiment of duty that can dominate the passions and hold steady sway against the temptations to vice, wrong doing, and destructive irregularities, without the quickening and supporting power of belief in a supreme ruler, is impossible. Atheistic ethical systems are practically impotent. They may present the ethical distinctions plainly, but their sanctions are gone. Enforcing motive power disappears when faith in a personal God is abandoned. Even common morality, in the ordinary plane of relationship between man and man in daily life, loses tone and nerve, and falls into corruption whenever touched by the breath of skepticism on this point. But more is true. If there be a God, man must sustain moral relations, that is, relations of duty, to Him; and the human virtue that takes no account of Him must be at best one-sided and defective. Thus all the high and unspeakable interests of morality are involved in the answer given to the question of the divine existence and government.

(3) To the *state* and civil prosperity Natural Theology is of equal importance. If theism is essential to both religion and morality, it is at once evident that it must be essential also to social order and national welfare. The testimony of history is emphatic, that a well ordered and prosperous state is an impossibility without it. So strongly has the experience of nations reflected this truth, that great statesmen have put it into the proposition that, were there no religion among a people one would have to be invented for state purposes. It is a very expressive fact in this connection, that in common law atheism is counted as disqualifying a witness in courts of justice. The truths of Natural Theology are therefore of vital moment to all the great interests of society and the state.

(4) They also concern *philosophy* and *science*. The theistic conception of the world is of necessity widely different from the atheistical conception of it. While the facts and phenomena of nature remain the same, the explanation of them, and their

relations and significance, become greatly changed. If theism and atheism must necessarily bear different fruits in religion and morals, they must also produce different systems of science and philosophy. They cannot, and do not, solve the problems of nature, life, and mind in the same way. These will always be found to depend very greatly on the position the scientist takes toward the truths which theology considers. The whole scientific system will take color from the light which falls upon it. He who finds in reason and nature clear evidence of a supreme intelligent First Cause, and he who finds there no proof of such Being—he who believes material force to be the potency and only source of all things, and he who believes that the universe originated and is ordered by an intelligent and self-existent Will, must inevitably look upon the world, life, history, and upon themselves so very differently, that the truth or falsity of the conclusions of theology becomes a matter of indisputable and momentous importance.

II. THE IDEA OF GOD—ITS CONTENT, GENESIS, AND ORIGINAL FORM

1. THE idea of God has been a variable conception, ranging from a very undefined impression of some Higher Power, as among barbarous tribes, to the distinct and developed conception of a Self-existent Personal Being, infinite in intelligence, power, and goodness, the First Cause, Maker, and Ruler of the universe, as found in the mind of the Christian philosopher and theologian. God is conceived of as the first principle, ground, and reason of all existence, not identical with the universe, but its Author, at once above and immanent in it.

Cudworth says: "The true and proper idea of God, in its most contracted form, is this: A being absolutely perfect."

Descartes defines the idea: "By the name of God I understand a substance infinite, eternal, immutable, independent, omniscient, almighty, by which myself and all other things that are have been created and produced."

Sir Isaac Newton: "The true God is a living, intelligent, powerful being, and from His other perfections it follows that He is supreme or most perfect. He is eternal and infinite, omnipotent and omniscient; that is, His duration reaches from eternity to eternity, His presence from infinity to infinity. He governs all things, and knows all things that are or can be done. He is not eternity and infinity, but eternal and infinite. He is not duration or space, but he endures and is present."

Dr. Henry N. Day, of New Haven: "God is an all-perfect being—one; real; of essential energy which is characterized as rational; absolute as to the grounds of His existence and action; infinite in duration, presence, and power; the source of all other being, and sovereign over all; and morally complete in holiness and blessedness."

Dr. B. F. Cocker, University of Michigan: "An unconditioned will, or self-directive power, seeing its own way, and having the reason and law of its action in itself alone."

These definitions will suffice to give the chief elements of the idea as it is now matured in Christian theism. How far it could have been developed by the mere light of nature it is impossible to determine. Perhaps Aristotle may be regarded as exhibiting the highest reach without revelation. But his statement: "God is a living being, eternal, most excellent, so that life and continuous and eternal duration of being belong to God," falls far short of the fullness of conception presented in Christian doctrine. But it is not necessary to settle this question here. For, while the idea, so filled and rounded out in consequence of the full light of revelation, has been developed into a form much beyond the possibilities of merely rational theology, the argument which Natural Theology proposes to conduct is equally valid upon a less complete conception. For its purposes the argument may, at the start, include in the idea of God no more than that of a Self-existent First Cause as the Creator and Ruler of the universe.

2. The genesis of the idea of God. How it first arose in the human mind, or fixed itself there, need not indeed be here settled. For it is not an essential point in the evidence of its truth. Yet it is of some importance, as certain theistic arguments gain or lose force according as one view or another is adopted on this point.

There is a class of explanations that may at once be justly set aside, both because of their intrinsic absurdity and because they are refuted in the end by the whole force of the theistic evidence. The explanations, often repeated, which assert, for instance, that the notion of deity is a phantom, born originally of ignorant human dread and fear in presence of the terrible and mysterious phenomena of nature; that it began in a superstitious reverence for natural forces; that it is a crafty invention of designing priests and rulers; that it arose from reverence for dead ancestors whom respect and affection elevated to divine position, all fall to pieces the moment earnest and philosophic inquiry is turned upon the subject. The atheistic theories of our day, with whatever learning and skill they have been elaborated, are found resolvable into reconstructions and modifications of these inadequate and futile hypotheses. A sufficient refutation of them comes in the fact that they all derive religion from the lower human faculties, and represent its object of worship as only a creation of ignorance and mistaken fear. How then is its permanence to be accounted for? What is due to trembling ignorance must die when ignorance dies. The specters of night must vanish when the day comes. But the conception of God has grown clearer and stronger as man has advanced in knowledge and science. The full radiance of the highest civilization has had no effect but to bring it up into purer and bolder distinctness and strength. The idea, concerning the validity of which Natural Theology inquires, is one which, whatever be its genesis and explanation, thus maintains its place and authority, and has grown most positive under the fullest light of science and culture. The explanations which credit it to the gross ignorance and phantom fears of an early condition of human savagery are thoroughly overthrown by the simple fact that the strength of theism belongs to the present age and the highest civilization.

But apart from these explanations, necessarily rejected by their utter insufficiency, there are three views that have been and may be held as to the origin of the idea.

First, that it originated through a *primitive revelation*. The first man or first men are supposed to have received a knowledge of God by direct supernatural disclosures of Himself and His will; and the various notions of a divine being, as found throughout the world, are looked upon as the broken and scattered rays of original revelation. The idea, thus given by special and immediate divine instruction, has been continued by tradition through all the ages and in all the branchings of the world-filling race. This view has been losing ground through the recent investigations and discussions of ethnology, philology, and comparative mythology. The discrediting of this explanation, however, is not necessarily a denial of a primitive revelation. It may readily be allowed that important supernatural instruction was given to the first human pair, furnishing the essential truths of religion, and that this knowledge was enlarged by repeated later communications. It is reasonable to believe that some rays of light thus given have reached into remotest places and may linger among many nations. But tradition has shown itself to be too uncertain an instrument to justify the belief that it has carried this truth into every tribe in which it is found, and has preserved it through all the darkness. The explanation seems insufficient to cover all the wide range of facts concerned. Moreover, it is not certain that though such revelation was given, the idea of God was entirely due to it or originated by it. It is doubtful whether it could have been more than the occasion of developing it; since in a divine manifestation at any time the human mind, it would seem, must at least identify *as* God the being who so reveals himself. Whatever may be the occasion of the birth of the idea, the idea of God must have its genesis *within* the mind, rising there in recognition of the Revealer. If there be a God as the author of the universe, nature itself becomes a revelation of Him. Probably, therefore, we dare not credit supernatural revelation, any more than natural, with being more than the occasion of the subjective genesis of the concept of God.

Secondly, that it has arisen *naturally and spontaneously* in the human soul. This explanation branches into two forms. One is that the idea of God is given to consciousness purely from what is within the mind—not simply an *a priori* necessary conviction, but one whose basis and developing force are wholly internal. It occurs when the soul looks down into the depths and contents of its own consciousness. This theory is illustrated in the view which traces it to a feeling of dependence and obligation, bringing the soul face to face with the divine. That to which the consciousness of dependence points is called God. Man, it is said, learns to pray before he learns to reason. "He feels within him," says Dean Mansel, "the consciousness of a Supreme Being, and the instinct of worship, before he can argue from effects to causes or estimate the traces of wisdom and benevolence scattered through the creation." Some have claimed that "there is a connection between God and the soul, as between light and the eye, sound and the ear, food and the palate." The other form of this explanation represents the idea as springing up in the mind under the suggestive power of the external universe. It is awakened, as an inference, through the mind's contemplation of nature, under the play of thought in the necessary action and reaction between reason and the external world. In the first of these forms, it is suggested by what the mind finds in itself; in the second, by what is external to it—from the revealing power of the great universe, speaking to us of its author. Whether the human soul, in its purely subjective data, would ever attain this so-called consciousness of God, is questionable. At least, no verification of the claim is possible, since no human consciousness can ever be found wholly destitute of knowledge of external objects, to report the possibilities of this inner source alone. Indeed, the consciousness itself awakes only under the stimulation of the sense-perceptions, and the intuitions become possible only in connection with knowledge of the material world. But there can hardly be the least doubt that there is something in the existence, order, structures, forces, and movements of the grand universe in which we are placed, and their kindling action on the rational faculties of intuition and inference, that tends to originate and develop the idea of God in the human soul when its faculties are mature and in normal healthy action.

 This general explanation, finding the genesis of the idea, not in a primitive revelation, but in the natural and necessary action of the mind as impressed by the works of creation, has the advantage of being in harmony with the great fact of man's unquestionably religious nature. He everywhere and in all ages appears with very original, profound, and almost ineradicable religious instincts and aptitudes. There is force in the statement that if man were dependent on a supernatural revelation for the idea of God, he would seem to have what Schelling has strikingly called "an original atheism of consciousness." This implication is avoided in finding the origin of the idea in the natural knowledge of mankind.

Thirdly, as these two sources are not necessarily antagonistic, they may concur, and probably have concurred in some degree, at least in some places, in forming the conception. If man enjoyed a primitive revelation, its light may have lingered in some regions in broken and faded rays, affording a starting point for the working of the human mind. In others the early light may have been lost, and men thrown upon purely natural resources. But whether looked upon as the remains of an original revelation or as a spontaneous natural conception, the idea would at first be exceedingly defective or hardly formed at all. No one man alone, no one generation alone, could have fully developed it and given it the completeness it now has, as apprehended in the full light of this Christian age. Our present idea of God, the sublimest and most impressive the human mind has, on *any* explanation of its origin, is a growth, with the development of long centuries in it. It has the fullness of a history in it. It has come to us rounded out and illuminated under the straining vision of countless generations of earnest souls "feeling after Him," and struggling into clearer and better conception. All the time, the works of creation, the events of history, and the light of revelation have been pouring their maturing radiance upon it. All this has made possible the idea as it now stands out in our Christian theism.

3. The earliest *Form* of the idea. The question here is whether it was polytheistic or monotheistic. The Positive Philosophy, formulated about fifty years ago, by Auguste Comte, and proceeding on the assumption that the human race necessarily develops through the three distinct stages or methods of thought and knowledge, the Theological, the Metaphysical, and the Positive, put down the earliest stage as theological. Dividing this earliest stage itself into three periods, it declared that religion began in Fetishism, passed then into Polytheism, and at length reached Monotheism. This marking of the first form as Fetishistic seems to have been adopted from De Brosses, a writer of Voltaire's day. It has been widely accepted and defended,

especially by writers who hold the evolutionist derivative origin of man from the lower animals. It represents the beginning of religion as consisting in the adoration or worship of the common objects of nature, animals, trees, streams, hills, or pieces of wood, as possessed of supernatural powers. Prof. Max Müller's examination of this hypothesis has cut it up by the roots, showing it to be utterly without support of facts, and intrinsically a gross misconception. The further claim of the scheme, that before religion reached the conception of one God it was polytheistic, worshipping many local, national, or tutelary divinities, has little more support than the theory of Fetishism, and is opposed by strong, and, we believe, decisive evidence. Polytheism credits the different parts and operations of nature to different and numerous supernatural beings; and it looks plausible when the unification of all natural causes into the will of one God is represented as marking, not the earliest, but a later and advanced stage of thought and development. The variety of the effects at first to be accounted for is supposed to lead, not only naturally, but necessarily, to an assumption of a variety of causes, and make the earliest idea of deity polytheistic. It is alleged that the historical evidence points to this; and that no trace of monotheism is to be found in the world except with a polytheism behind it. It is by no means certain, however, that the natural or necessary movement of the mind, on the first impressions from nature, impressions often, doubtless, very general, and from viewing it in confused mass, would be to an immediate multiplication of the difficult conception of divine existence. The unity of nature is about as obtrusive a fact as is its variety. Moreover, "no human mind could conceive the idea of gods without having previously conceived the idea of a god." The singular, in thought as in language, precedes the plural. And the results of the latest and best critical, philological, archæological, and historical research point strongly to a primitive monotheism, and to subsequent obscurations of the idea of one God by applications of it to local, national and specific relations. They bring out the fact that while the early literature of the various nations of the Aryan or Indo-European family exhibits a multitudinous polytheism, it becomes simpler the further it is traced back. "The younger the polytheism the fewer the gods." When the names for God, as found in all the later or existing branches of this race, are examined and compared—as the Sanscrit *Dyaus*, the Greek *Zeus*, the Latin *Ju*, in Jupiter, the Gothic *Tius*, the Anglo-Saxon *Tiw*, the Scandinavian *Tyr*, the old German *Ziu* or *Zio*—they are found to have a common root from the old home where the race once dwelt together, before their dispersions or migrations. So that "in the period that lay behind the Homeric poems and the *Vedas* and the earliest Gothic and Scandinavian legends, when Greek and Roman, Indian, Celt, and Teuton were still a single people, a single name for God was in use." We are entitled to accept with much confidence the conclusion of Prof. Max Müller, who says: "If an expression had been given to that primitive intuition of the deity, it would have been 'There is a God,' but not yet 'There is but one God.' The latter form of faith, the belief in one God, is properly called monotheism, whereas the term henotheism would best express the faith in a single God."[2] This "henotheism "designates the initial form of unity, before there had been yet joined with it a distinct negation of more than one, and when the same infinite, invisible power was worshipped under different names drawn from the chief objects that seemed to reveal its presence. This, and not polytheism, Max Müller finds to be the earliest form in India and other countries. As to Egypt, where are found records among the most ancient of any in the world, M. Emanuel Rougé says: "The first characteristic of the religion is the unity of God, most energetically expressed: God, One, Sole, and Only; no others with Him. He is the only Being living in truth." P. Le Page Renouf, also an accredited Egyptologist, adds confirmatory testimony, and tells of texts in the early mythology of that country, "wherein Rā, Osiris, Amon, and all other gods disappear, except as simple *names*, and the unity of God is asserted in the noblest language of monotheistic religion." As to China, where again we have one of our deepest openings into antiquity, James Legge, Professor of the Chinese language and literature in the University of Oxford, one of the most competent witnesses, says of the several primitive words for God: "The two characters show us the religion of the ancient Chinese as a monotheism.... Five thousand years ago, the Chinese were monotheists—not henotheists, but monotheists—and this monotheism was in danger of being corrupted."

Similar interpretations of the indications in the earliest religions of the race might be quoted from other authorities. They make it fair to suppose that the monotheistic form was the most ancient, and that polytheism represents corruptions of it. Polytheistic mythologies are broken lights.

4. The relation of this idea of God to the aim of Natural Theology. It furnishes the starting point for the argument as to the divine existence and character. The aim of the discussion is to show the validity of the idea, or prove the real existence of the Being for whom this idea stands in the human mind. It proposes to show that it is not an empty phantom and delusion, a false impression and misleading dream, but represents a necessary and grand reality.

Natural Theology

PART I

EVIDENCES OF THE DIVINE EXISTENCE

SINCE the proofs of God's existence must be the manifestations He has given of Himself, they must be as varied and numerous as are the phenomena of the whole world of mind and matter, on which He has imprinted His power and thought, and which are now open to our knowledge through perception, consciousness, and reason. The universe in all its matter, mind, and history, presents the pages of the great volume of His self-disclosure. If there be a God as creator and sovereign of all, then all must speak of Him. The theistic evidences must, therefore, be literally countless, and be found in all the powers, movements, laws, and relations of both organic and inorganic nature, and the whole realm of human mind and history. No one source of evidence excludes another, no legitimate reasoning process shuts off the right of any other intrinsically sound process, or makes it useless. Each one of these countless evidences and processes may furnish its own separate and legitimate testimony, and this testimony may be reflected in a thousand different ways to different minds. It is fair to assume that if there is a single evidence, there are many evidences. If there is one, there are myriad points of light, revealing the divine. In their individual and separate force, many of these evidences may fall short of a full proof. Some of them, however, under the necessities of logical thought and according to principles or laws of evidence held as fully sufficient to establish truth in any of the sciences, may, even in their individual and single force, carry the conclusion legitimately up to the grade of satisfactory proof. But the full proof is to be found in no one argument or source of argument alone. The evidences are in the largest and truest sense cumulative. "They concur and unite into a single all-comprehensive argument, which is just the sum of all the indications of God discoverable in all departments of nature, thought, and history." It is only when all realms have been examined, when all special arguments and separate evidences are brought together and looked upon in their concurrent testimony, each corroborating and supporting the others and joining its logical demand for the same conclusion, that the theistic proof swells into its real and legitimate force. The full proof is not in one thing, or only a few things, or in one sort of argument alone, but in the bearing and trend, the implications and demands of numberless things, the consilience and accumulation of manifold separate and independent evidences.

Attention needs to be called to this because some theistic writers have rested the entire proof on a single kind of evidence, disparaging or discrediting all other arguments. Not unfrequently, for instance, misled by the plausible teaching of an unsound philosophy, they have denied the validity and value of the whole physico-theological argument, and, with Kant, found the true proof only in the moral evidence, or with others, only in an immediate consciousness of God. We cannot but think that this restriction of the theistic proof to but one argument or only several, is utterly unwarranted, and as harmful as it is foolish. When the truth is thus unwisely and wrongly made to rest on such limited and perhaps obscure ground, the impression is naturally created in superficial men, that its foundations are very meagre and insecure. Any doubt raised on the remaining evidence throws them into helpless skepticism. Well-meaning and earnest supporters of theistic truth have often given aid and advantage to its enemies, and wrought in the interest of unbelief by this mistaken procedure. Scarcely less unwise and less harmful has this been than the position assumed by some Christian believers, that the existence of God, though a great truth, is a truth that does not admit of proof at all, but is to be accepted by faith alone on the information of revelation. These go so far as to assume that "God has left himself without witness," except in these Scriptures, and appear to take no account of the teaching of these Scriptures themselves, that "the heavens declare the glory of God and the firmament shows His handiwork," and that "the invisible things of Him, from the creation of the world, are clearly seen, being understood by the things which are made." And if the universe of the things which are made manifests His being anywhere, it must naturally and justly be understood to manifest it everywhere. A thousand points of the divine operation would have to be rubbed out before He could be hid from view, or the forthshining of His existence and character entirely clouded. Much poor reasoning in the service of theism might be shown to be poor, without at all seriously weakening the aggregate of valid evidence.

In general, *two methods* of proof have been recognized and used in theistic argument. They are the two generic methods acknowledged in logic. One is the *a priori* method, the other the *a posteriori*. According to its most ancient Aristotelian sense, *a priori* reasoning is that which proceeds from cause to effect or antecedent to consequent. In modern times its sense has been modified and its application extended, so as to include any abstract reasoning from what are known as *a priori* or necessary truths, to the conditions which such first-truths involve. As now employed, it is reasoning from any general principles, held to be self-evident, to their applications. The *a posteriori* method, on the contrary, begins with observed facts and phenomena, and tracing them backward, arrives at a knowledge of their cause. It is from effect to cause, from observed facts to a general principle, from facts of experience to realities which must condition experience. But this distinction, theoretically clear, between these two methods, becomes practically loose and uncertain. Neither method remains pure, or can be pursued alone in actual argument, but each employs somewhat of the other. They run together and unite, so that it is often difficult to determine which predominates or is the characteristic method.

These two methods have given us the two great and leading forms of theistic proof—the *a priori* method giving the *ontological* proof, the *a posteriori*, the *physico-theological*. As, however, the physico-theological proof is twofold, naturally separating into the so-called cosmological and the teleological, and there are evidences not conveniently included in this division, and as the *a priori* and *a posteriori* methods, when brought into actual use, so unite and blend that they fail to classify the several arguments distinctly, we will, for better arrangement, gather the different evidences under the following heads: I. PRESUMPTIVE EVIDENCES; II. THE ONTOLOGICAL EVIDENCE; III. THE COSMOLOGICAL EVIDENCE; IV. THE TELEOLOGICAL EVIDENCE; V. THE MORAL EVIDENCE.

CHAPTER I

PRESUMPTIVE EVIDENCE

THERE are various considerations that, while not amounting to complete proofs, are yet so forcibly suggestive as at once to throw strong presumptions on the side of theism. They do not, indeed, demonstrate its truth, but, appearing as the first indications on the very face of the subject, as it presents itself for examination, they not only prepare the way for the more direct and positive proofs, but give us the evident and strong probabilities from the start—probabilities which ought to be held as of even decisive weight unless set aside by contrary proofs. They show the clear trend of the whole question. These considerations are naturally placed as the initial evidences for the Divine Existence.

1. The first of these is the *universality of the idea of God* in the human mind. Historical and ethnological researches, carried on in late years with great earnestness and care, fully justify the statement that this idea is connatural to man. Its prevalence is justly held as universal. Wherever the human mind has had its normal and healthy unfolding, the idea has appeared. We are safe in saying that there has been found no well authenticated case of a nation or race utterly without some conception of deity or conviction of the existence of a Supreme Being. It is true that, looking on the low state of barbarous tribes with the most unfavorable preconceptions, and perhaps unwilling to believe any knowledge of God possible except from revelation, missionaries and travellers have sometimes reported different peoples, in

India, China, Australia, and Africa, as wholly without any idea of a Divine Being or a word to express the idea. But further inquiry and better knowledge of their language, literature and life have invariably shown such conclusions to have been hasty and erroneous. Even among the lowest tribes are found objects of worship, to which divine powers are supposed to belong.

It is no exception to this universality, that in many places the idea is exceedingly crude, gross, and even grotesque and false. For at the best, man's conception of God is imperfect, and it is confessedly reached by different peoples in very different degrees of clearness and correctness. In the dense fogs of barbarism, where hardly a trace of the divine image in man remains, the divine above him, if discerned at all, would necessarily appear only as an obscure, shifting, gloomy, and perhaps frightful, phantom. In such low ignorance no truth of any sort is seen except in broken forms or pale shadows. Spiritual conceptions are simply as crude as the knowledge of other great realities. Nor is it to be counted a fair exception, when we are pointed to Buddhism with its hundreds of millions of adherents, and to the so-called atheism which, in the midst of our Christian civilization, parades in the assumed name of philosophy, science and culture. These phenomena present no real conflict with the truth here maintained. For as to Buddhism, the assertion that it is utterly atheistic is more than doubted by eminent students of its literature. Buddhism undoubtedly rose on the basis of the Brahmanic philosophy, and this was fundamentally monotheistic, and held to the existence of "an Absolute and Supreme Being as the source of all that exists." *Brahm* was "pure intelligence," "sole and self-existent," the creator. *Buddha* means the same—"absolute light," "perfect wisdom." In denying the existence of the "devas "or gods with which a polytheistic corruption had overlaid Brahmanism, Buddhism did not necessarily deny this supreme intelligence. The overthrow of polytheistic worships usually marks an advance of a purer and truer theism. Max Müller, therefore, may be right in saying: "They threw away the old names, but they did not throw away their belief in that which they tried to name. After destroying the altars of their old gods, they built out of the scattered bricks a new altar to the Unknown

God."[3] That Buddhism has its temples and worship and prayers does not point toward an utter atheism. Even should it in fact deny the real existence of any God other than the aggregate intelligence and order of the world, this very denial confesses to the presence of the rejected conception as still revealing itself in the mind. As to the atheism found in Christian lands, the exception is only apparent. Besides being so inconsiderable as to owe its notoriety mainly to the shock and offence it gives to the ruling convictions of men, it strikingly fails to escape the necessity and grasp of the idea it claims to reject. Its appearance is not normal or spontaneous, but the result of either speculative difficulties or perverted moral inclinations. It probably never amounts to a positive intellectual conviction, but is simply the negative state of doubt or unbelief. And evidence is not wanting that both the intellect and the heart recoil from every atheistic conclusion. For the necessities of thought and the demands of the profoundest forces of life continually throw men back on some religious positions even when they have supposed themselves freed from them. When they have pushed God out from one door, a god is found to have entered at another. They have speculated and contended concerning "the essence of the primal existence" and the first cause of the universe, but even those who have most positively rejected belief in God as the Personal Author of nature, have straightway proceeded to make a god of Force, or of the Atom, or of Law, transferring to it both creatorship and sovereignty. Thus the so-called atheist of our day has usually only shifted the position and changed the form of the idea, and often falls back into a deification of the powers or attributes of nature and some worship of an idealized humanity or of the universe. So persistent is the conception of deity. Not only has the human mind shown no repugnance to it, but has developed or accepted it as natural and normal. It maintains itself in all ages and in all nations, presenting one of the most universal convictions of the race.

Now, whatever theory we may adopt as to the origin of this conviction, its wonderful prevalence becomes a strong presumption of its truth. If held to be due to a primitive revelation, the existence of God who revealed Himself is at once acknowledged. If it be regarded as arising naturally and spontaneously from the mind itself, under impressions from nature, the universality and ruling strength of the belief become a clear and strong presumption of its truth. For a conviction that springs so inevitably from experience and the action of reason in the presence of the phenomena of the world, and is so perennial in vitality, is justly viewed as founded on reality. That an idea should be so thoroughly normal to the human mind as this has proved to be, forcing itself into recognition everywhere and in all ages, asserting a virtual omnipresence in the thought and belief of the race under all conditions and changes, and yet be wholly false and illegitimate, a universal but necessary mistake, is against all natural and reasonable probability. We justly see something more than a dream and delusion in such a universal, free, and unconquerable conviction. Especially so, if we add to this impressive prevalence the ever-felt necessity of it, for the welfare of life and the order of society. While it has appeared everywhere, it has only met a fundamental and plain need of the race. It has only furnished what is known to be required for man's moral nature and the restraint of wrong. With its accompanying convictions of obligation and responsibility, it has come as an indispensable force for duty and good character, for the proper well-being and best development of humanity. All this looks like the signature of truth.

2. A second evidence of this kind is the *religious instinct* of the race. This is properly mentioned separately here, because it presents another fact of man's constitution. In connection with the idea of God, so universally found, there is a further principle, everywhere showing itself in religious feeling and acts of worship. Apparently even deeper than that idea, are the feelings of dependence and need, the tendencies to reverence and homage, and the craving for some fellowship with divine powers above man. We may rightly call all this a religious instinct, as it evidently comes out of the very framework and set of the mental and moral sensibilities. In heart, as well as in intellect, man's nature shows an organization for religion, an adaptation and impulse toward it so decided and influential as to reveal itself everywhere.

Religious sentiments and proclivities have been found in all nations and tribes. Worship offered to a Supreme Being, or some divinity supposed to control the welfare and destiny of man, has been coeval and coextensive with the race. Every people, not purely monotheistic, is found to have a mythology, and each mythologic system has been but the attempt to give formal expression to the relations which are felt to connect men with invisible supernatural powers. The literature of every land, where a literature has been discovered at all, reveals the coloring of the religious sentiments; the customs and habits of wholly illiterate tribes are usually deeply and unmistakably marked by their action. However degraded the savagery, or blind and distorted the impulse, the instinct has been there. It changes its manifestations, but never disappears. Everywhere there have been temples, or oracles, or offerings, or sacrifices, prayers, vows, or other acts of worship.

The religious principle or sentiment in man has been as powerful as certain. It has woven itself in with the entire structure of human society and life, and has run its clear lines through every system of thought and philosophy, from the rudest to the most elaborate and refined. At no point has human nature been more sensitive, or more ready to reveal powers of intense and emphatic action. While usually the religious instincts and ideas have been the support and defense of prevalent forms of government and society, they have often, especially when either assailed or quickened by new light, swept institutions from their foundations and revolutionized life.

One of the surest forms in which this religious constitution is revealed is in the soul's conscious cravings for a higher fellowship than with the finite, visible beings around it. The soul carries with it a constant sense of dependence. It feels a need of support and guidance by some stronger hand. It has aspirations that look to and crave communion with what is above it. It is restless, unless it can rest itself in the bosom of some all-embracing protection, fellowship, and care. The human heart must have a God, as truly as must the mind develop the idea of one. It has struggled to reach His favor and get hold of His hand, feeling after Him, if perchance it might find Him, through sacrifices, prayers, and vows, in protracted meditations and mystic ceremonies. So, by a natural necessity, manifold systems and forms of religion have been developed. The strong words of Dr. Day well sum up this truth: "The dependent, finite, human soul craves the absolute and the infinite. It craves a sympathy that outreaches all that is not truly independent and unlimited, and will not be satisfied till it finds that which is adequate to meet not only the limited actualities, but the infinite possibilities of its need and its condition, and is high uplifted above all that *can* condition, that can hamper or extinguish. It craves communion with a craving which no finite soul can satisfy, with a higher and a higher, even with a highest, toward which it may ever be rising, but which it can never reach.... It craves, in its instinctive aspirations for truth that pant for more than they obtain, an object that is without exhaustion, of illimitable vastness and incalculable richness. It craves, in the felt darkness about it, a light and a wisdom that is beyond all possibility of failing. It craves, in its sense of weakness which necessarily attaches to it as dependent, a help and supply of strength that can be relied on in any of the infinite possibilities of its experience."

If it be said that there are persons who have no such consciousness of religious wants, it is enough to reply that these cases are manifestly exceptional and abnormal, even as there are many persons who, through a false or defective development, fail to present various other undoubtedly natural parts of full manhood, as, *e.g.*, conscience and love of the beautiful. If it be alleged that antipathies to religion also appear in human nature, and that many men, when developed under the large culture of science and philosophy, hasten, as if under a strong aversion to it, to reject all belief in God and the supernatural, and exhibit feelings intensely anti-religious, the following considerations deserve to be kept in mind: *First*, it may be freely conceded that human nature exhibits some feelings and impulses at war with the truths and life of religion. It is not claimed that it has no forces that run counter to these religious instincts. It is even too true that there are discords in it. *Secondly*, the religious aptitudes manifestly belong to its deeper and more constitutive elements, and so are justly considered as original and truly genuine. The antagonistic forces seem to be in no sense necessary, and therefore primitively and truly natural, as the religious instinct plainly shows itself to be. And *thirdly*, even when the idea of God is theoretically discarded and religion rejected, the force of the original adaptation and affinity for religion, refusing to be wiped utterly out, is wont to reassert itself in the very face of the denial. Conspicuous instances illustrate how human nature throws back the deniers of religion into acknowledgment of religion. Auguste Comte, who built his philosophic theory on atheism and a denial of all religious verities, in the end, led by his own emotional nature which his system had defrauded, appended his scheme deifying ideal humanity and establishing a system of worship and rites. Though he rejected religion in the beginning, the necessities of worship of some sort forced the manufacture of a new religion at the last. Materialism and materialistic philosophies are found returning upon their own paths in this respect. Unwilling or unable to discern any God in the universe or any spiritual existence in man, not believing in any future life or any supernatural powers, recognizing the existence of only force and matter evolving all physical and mental phenomena, they yet, in the end, not only consent to the fact of the religious necessities of human nature, but proceed to tell how it may still worship when God is denied and both freedom and responsibility are theoretically destroyed. Failing by their theories to eradicate the religiousness that lies in the very depth of the soul's constitution, they invite it to exercise the religious sensibilities in reverence, homage, and trust in nature, in the universe, as the highest form of power. The idea of God is replaced by that of the Cosmos. "We demand," say Strauss, Haeckel, Oscar Schmidt, and others, in substance, "we demand the same piety for our Cosmos that the devout of old demanded for his God." Prof. Tyndall was therefore right, when, in his famous Belfast address, though believing that the potency of all things might be found in matter, he yet conceded that man's religious instincts and necessities could not be justly denied or overlooked.

What is the meaning of all this? To what do these instincts look? Do these deep cravings reach out forever only into blank vacancy and to nothingness? Are they presenting these prayers, this gratitude, this confidence where there is no Being at all to hear? Is this necessary worship, clustering around this necessary idea of God, only the acting out of a necessary dream? Is there really no Father in heaven at all, whose hand these needy children are seeking to find and believing they do find? These deep and abiding instincts must imply the existence of the Divine Being, unless human nature be fundamentally false. That it is thus false, it is utterly unreasonable to believe. For one of the most incontestable facts, established by observation and inductive science, is that every well defined instinct, wherever found, implies and points to its corresponding reality. Whatever theory as to the origin of things men may adopt, they recognize the fact that a law of adjustment and correspondency everywhere prevails. Nature makes no halves, leaves no parts standing alone, presents no monstrosities of structure in which subjective constitutional cravings and necessities are left without external complement or supply. The eye is answered by the light, the ear by the atmosphere, the lungs by the air, the appetite by food; over against the intellect, and fitting it, are the objects of knowledge; the sensibilities find their subjects ready for them; the will looks out on a real field of voluntary action. Passing on to the instincts, the certainty of their indications and directive action has ever been one of the things for wonder and admiration. As far as scientifically examined, they are not misleading. Whether they teach the bee to construct its cell, or the beaver its house, or the bird its nest, whether they inform the pigeon of the time and way of its migration, or direct the fishes to the distant waters to deposit their eggs, they are all followed safely. They do not mock or point to nothing. Every positive normal instinct expresses a truth and looks to a reality far beyond itself, pointing out that reality through the darkness with almost unerring ray. Not more truly does the lake, reflecting stars from its deep bosom, certify the reality of the starry heavens above it, than do these universal instincts assure the objects which we behold mirrored in them. To look upon the deep *religious* human instincts alone as deceptive and spurious would be utterly unreasonable and unscientific. They therefore form a clear and valid presumption for the real existence of the Infinite Supreme Being whom they necessarily imply. "It would be irrational in the last degree to lay down the existence of such a need and such a tendency, and yet believe that the need corresponds to nothing, that the tendency has no goal. Religious history, by bringing clearly into light the universality, the persistency, and the prodigious intensity of religion in human life, is, therefore, to my mind, one unbroken attestation of God."

3. The *benign influence* of belief in God is a natural sign of its truth. Though utility and truth are different conceptions, and utility does not make truth, yet it often serves to prove it and helps to find it. For, to a degree that has made the fact both clear and impressive, truth is promotive of man's welfare and happiness, while error misleads and blights. Falsehood kills like frost every precious thing it touches. The channels of error can bear no refreshing streams for virtue, life, order, or happiness. But truth is light, sunshine, and blessed power to the world. It is health and vigor to the mind. It is elevation and progress to society and every human interest. Now, belief in the existence and government of a Supreme Being has the clear testimony of utility. The ideas of God, responsibility, divine favor and divine displeasure, have unquestionably been potent for justice, veracity, honesty, temperance, purity, and order. They have tended to repress wrong. They have given nerve to moral character. Neither individuals nor communities could afford to be without their help. Long before the days of Plutarch, who wrote: "I am of opinion that a city might sooner be built without any ground to fix it on than a commonwealth be constituted together without any religion or idea of the Gods, or, being constituted, be preserved," moralists had been feeling that neither personal life nor society could bear the loss of this faith. In all ages since, it has proved to be the only truly granite foundation for virtue and social order. And this strength of benign influence has always been in direct proportion to the clearness and fullness of the theistic faith. Prevailingly, indeed, the idea of the Supreme Being has been so overlaid by distorting polytheisms, and His relations to the world and man have been so shrouded in darkness and error as to turn the true fruit in large measure into false. Often the notion of God has been so dreadfully misconceived as to

pervert religion into conflict with even morality, and make it a wasting power. But this is a result that attends the falsification of any great and potent truth. The blight becomes proportionate to the greatness of the truth perverted. But whenever the conception of God has been clear and well developed, discerning Him as the self-existent Maker and Governor of the universe, infinite in power, wisdom, and goodness, and especially as the Father of all, then this faith quickens and strengthens all the best forces of human life and purifies and elevates all its joys. Not only does it carry virtue, but carries it with a richness proportioned to the depth and fullness of its conception of the Divine Being. The best and loftiest ethical systems the world has ever known are found under the light of the clearest and most positive theism. Under this light the human mind shows its healthiest vigor, the conscience its clearest affirmations and its most regal authority. Under it manhood grows to its noblest forms and shows its finest possibilities. Under it science and philosophy are achieving their grandest successes, culture is bearing its richest fruits, and nations are growing the freest and strongest.

The relation of faith in God to the nourishment and vigor of our moral nature deserves to be specially emphasized. There may, indeed, be some morality without religion, as the sense of right and wrong is, to some degree at least, spontaneous and necessary. Atheism may even construct a sort of ethical system. But attempts to explain the origin of the world and man on atheistic hypotheses have really found no just foundation for either freedom and responsibility or the authority of conscience. The effort of Herbert Spencer, after having only removed the idea of God into the dark realm of the "unknowable," has become conspicuous chiefly by its evident failure. In it the ideas of right and wrong have fallen away, and only those of utility and pleasure remain. While, on the one hand, faith in an almighty Maker and Ruler, holy, good, and righteous, is naturally a fountain of health and strength to the moral sentiment and principles, it is unquestionable, on the other hand, that atheistic opinions practically tend to relax the moral life of both men and communities. They cut the nerves of conscience. They put out the lights, or lower them to an ineffectual glimmer. The theoretical atheists of a community are never its moral glory. They do not carry its inspiring or uplifting forces. No man ever gains virtuous strength and purity by loss of faith in God. Almost everyone, by such loss, drops down into inferior character. It was hardly without some relation of cause and effect that the crimes and horrors with which the first French Revolution appalled mankind came out from beneath the lifted banner of atheism. It is a simple fact that at the present time, wherever materialism or other speculative theories have overthrown belief in God, demoralization sets in like a fast rot. Anarchic forces are unchained. It is by no accident that atheism has gotten the further name of nihilism—the term that stands for the most conscienceless plans and frightful crimes that are now illustrating the capabilities of human depravity. It is not chance that finds the most dangerous of the "dangerous classes" to be atheists. It must be admitted, indeed, that simple belief in God does not stay all wrongs, and sometimes atrocious and horrible crimes have been committed in the very name of religion, as in cruel wars for its propagation and in frequent persecutions. It is proper to mention this, because some people may think of it not simply as an exception to the good influence of theistic belief, which it possibly is, but as a contradiction or disproof of it, which it plainly is not; for it is in no sort a necessary or logical result of the belief. But it is manifestly a violent and gross perversion of its true and rightful influence, and comes from the bad passions of men which often seize and use in unreasonable and violent way the holiest truths. It is grossly absurd to credit to any truth whatever the consequences which flow from men's violation of it. And this incidental result, as a perversion, has been only occasional, while the normal working influence has ever been the benign, quickening, uplifting, fructifying force for the best, strongest, most unselfish and happy life of which the world knows. And this is a strong presumption of its truth. It is hardly a falsehood that bears these happy fruits, a thorn that bears these grapes.

    4. All the facts, phenomena, and appearances of the world are best explained and harmonized under the belief of the existence of God. No principle of scientific procedure is more fully

recognized than that a theory is proved true by its thoroughly interpreting and accounting for all the phenomena concerned. When a supposition or doctrine works badly it is discredited as out of harmony with the nature of things. If it explains and solves all the elements involved, it gains scientific authority. Thus a conjecture as to the sun's true place in the solar system passed from the rank of a supposition to that of science, in heliocentric astronomy. So, too, a hypothesis of Newton's mind has become the scientific law of gravitation. As it explains all the phenomena, it is accredited as true, despite the fact that gravitation itself is inscrutable.

The doctrine of God affords the most direct interpretation of all the phenomena of nature, and the *only* explanation yet found for many of them. Besides such facts as have been already mentioned, viz.: the prevalent conception of a divine existence, the religious nature of man, and the beneficent influence of theistic belief, there are numberless things in the constitution of nature, and in human experience, which are most readily accounted for, as mankind has shown a strong tendency to account for them, by this doctrine. And there are not a few things that have hitherto baffled all other solution. The existence of matter and its forces—or of force and matter, should anyone prefer this way of statement—in marvelous adaptation to world-building and organization, science must, apart from this doctrine, simply *assume* without explanation. The origin of life, the origin of sensation, the genesis of consciousness, self-consciousness, and moral self-determination, are all inscrutable before every attempt of science. With its most searching light it has neither found nor shown a bridge of transition from lifelessness to life, from mere matter to sensation, from sensation to free will and the appearance of self-determining personality. It lacks reasonable answer to the question of origin on all these points, and unless it consents to let them remain unaccounted for, must still toil on in the baffling inquiry. It may not be legitimate, at this stage of the discussion and evidence, to claim, what the facts might indeed logically justify, that life, consciousness, personality, and a moral nature in themselves prove the existence of God. But we may fairly maintain that the direct solution which the doctrine of an infinite, living, intelligent Creator furnishes to these otherwise insoluble problems, is an almost decisive presumption in its favor. Taken in connection with the unquestionable fact that it furnishes a direct and reasonable explanation of all the phenomena of the universe of mind and matter, it is scientifically accredited as truth. To use the words of an able thinker and writer: "It is not rash to say that it is beyond all comparison stronger as a hypothesis which accounts for all phenomena under it than any accepted theory in the science of the physical universe in any department—than that of heat, or light, of primeval atoms, or of gravity itself." "The simplest conception which explains and connects the phenomena," writes Prof. Henry, of the Smithsonian Institution, "is that of the existence of one spiritual Being, infinite in wisdom, power, in all divine perfections, which exists always and everywhere."

It is no sufficient answer to this strong presumption for theism from its affording a clear solution of all the phenomena of the world, to bring forward, as is sometimes done, the difficulty of conceiving of a self-existent Being, a Being unoriginated and eternal. This is probably the chief difficulty sought to be escaped by atheistic theories. The existence of God, it is said, needs as much to be accounted for as the universe itself. But it is enough to point out that, at the worst, a self-existent God is no more difficult to conceive of than a self-existent universe. The great mystery of self-existence, or of eternally existent being, is not escaped by denial of a God. It must be admitted *somewhere*. For, since something now exists, something must always have existed; for it is impossible that something should arise out of nothing, or being should spring uncaused out of non-being. Present existence is full proof that *something* has existed from eternity. This is conceded by all—atheists as well as theists. The question, therefore, resolves itself into this: Which is the more reasonable supposition—that an unintelligent force or matter has produced this universe of worlds, with masses, distances, and movements in exactest harmony, filled with beneficent adaptations, marvellous organisms, and millions on millions of rational and moral beings, or that one intelligent, self-existent, almighty Being has planned and created it all? Nothing in the world itself, with its ever changing forms and dependent existences, suggests the qualities of necessity and self-existence in its own nature. To substitute a self-existence of the universe, with its incalculable multiplicity of parts and interdependencies, and countless actual human personalities, for the self-existence of God, multiplies the mystery a thousand-fold. The self-existence of God, therefore, offers less difficulty than the self-existence of the world. It is a reduction of the mystery to its lowest terms, to absolute unity and simplicity. It is therefore scientific, and challenges acceptance by its being the most reasonable.

CHAPTER II

THE ONTOLOGICAL EVIDENCE

THIS is an application of the *a priori* method of proof. Ontology, from ὤν, ὄντος, *being*, and λόγος *discourse*, designates the study which investigates the reality, nature, and relations of *being as such*. It agrees with the term "metaphysics," as occupied with inquiries into the essence of things and the validity of our knowledge. As a term for a mode of theistic proof, "ontological" is used almost synonymously with the term *"a priori,"* and designates that kind or way of argument which starts, not with the facts of sense-experience or observed phenomena of the world, but with ideas which are held as intuitive and necessary in the mind's own insight, and the primary and universal principles and laws of thought. Out of these it seeks to show the necessary existence of an infinite, absolute, intelligent, and eternal Being.

While marked by the characteristic of always proceeding from the internal idea to the necessary existence of God, this *a priori* or ontological proof is found in a great variety of forms. It belongs chiefly to modern times, and has been shaped into many different and distinct arguments. We do not lay great stress upon it as a separate and independent proof, or as a form of demonstration, viewed in its own terms alone. Though sometimes claimed to be *the* proof, complete and sufficient in itself, we are compelled to regard it, when taken alone in any and all of the forms in which it has been constructed, as one of the least satisfactory and serviceable of the theistic proofs. Apart from serious defects usually found in it, it is too metaphysical to carry strong conviction. Whatever force it may have to some minds, highly disciplined in abstract thought, it is necessarily almost, if not wholly, useless with the masses of men. They do not, and cannot, comprehend its abstract terms, nor see or feel the force of the subtle logic that links, or seems to link, these terms to each other and to the conclusion. But while as a distinct and independent argument, it is of less value, we think, than is often claimed for it, it is not to be set aside or held as of no account. For in the necessary judgments and first principles of the mind, which it brings to view, it unquestionably furnishes some initial as well as completing elements needed for the *a posteriori* or physico-theological evidences. In the intuitive perceptions of the reason, whose ideas and implications it seeks to trace under the laws of logical thought, it supplies the judgments which crown and confirm all the great proofs. It will be enough, at this point—and probably the best way to explain it—to place before the reader the substance of some of the chief forms in which it has been presented.

1. The germs of it appear in Plato. His view can be understood only in connection with his theory of "ideas." The universe, he taught, includes more than the sensible world. We find *ideas* also in it. These ideas are the archetypal realities, original and permanent, while all visible and material things are only the temporary and fleeting forms in which they come into passing manifestation. It is only by apprehension of these "ideas" that we know the true realities reflected in the phenomena of the world. They do not originate in material things, but are before them, and belong to *mind.* Yet they are not created by *our* minds, which merely apprehend and receive them. They come to us. They must, therefore, belong to a higher Mind, and subsist in primal and permanent reality in the Infinite Reason whose thoughts are reflected in nature. The idea of a Supreme Mind is in our minds only because of the real existence of the Being it represents, and becomes a direct proof of such Being. Plato, it must be remembered, did not definitely formulate an argument in this way, but his philosophy is found to contain the underlying principles which naturally come together in such argument, and

which started and guided subsequent thinkers. They appear in Augustine and among theologians generally since.

2. *Anselm*, archbishop of Canterbury, 1093–1109, with whom the ontological argument properly begins, rested it upon the idea of a most perfect Being. It was, in substance: "The human mind possesses the idea of the most perfect Being conceivable. But such a Being is *necessarily existent;* because a being whose existence is contingent, who may or may not exist, is not the most perfect being of which we can conceive. Being can be conceived to exist in reality also, and this is something greater. Hence, the most perfect must exist not simply in the intellect, but in the sphere of objective reality. God, therefore, is not simply conceived by us; He really exists."

3. *Descartes*, who uses several *a posteriori* arguments, gives also an ontological proof which has been condensed as follows: "On analyzing the idea we have of God as the most real Being, containing every perfection, I find that *existence* must be comprised among these perfections, otherwise the idea could be enlarged by adding this quality, which is absurd. In other ideas existence is not such a necessary ingredient, because they are not considered as unique and absolutely perfect. But in this existence must be comprised. Hence the very idea of God, rightly understood, includes in it necessary existence, and the existence of the Deity is proved from the very fact that we possess a notion of Him."

4. Bishop *Butler* presents the ontological proof thus: "We find within ourselves the idea of infinity, *i.e.*, immensity and eternity, impossible, even in imagination, to be removed out of being. We seem to discern intuitively that there must and cannot but be somewhat external to ourselves, answering this idea, or the archetype of it. And hence (for *this abstract*, as much as any other, implies a concrete) we conclude that there is, and cannot but be, an infinite and immense eternal Being existing, prior to all design contributing to His existence, and exclusive of it."

5. The statement of the reasoning given by *Cousin*, is a fair example: "The idea of God," says he, "is a primitive idea; but whence does this idea come to you? Is it a creation of your imagination, an illusion, a chimera? You can imagine a gorgon, a

centaur, to exist, and you can imagine them not to exist; but is it in your power, the finite and imperfect being given, to conceive or not to conceive the infinite and the perfect? No, the one being given, the other is necessary. It is not, then, a chimera; it is a necessary product of your reason; therefore it is a legitimate product. Being a legitimate product, it must point to a reality. Else you make your reason dishonest and false.... You are a finite being, and you have the necessary idea of an infinite being. But how could a finite and imperfect being have the idea of an infinite and perfect being, and have it necessarily, if this being did not exist?... The single fact of the conception of God by reason, the idea, alone, of God, implies the certainty and the necessity of the existence of God."

6. We omit account of the different forms given to the argument by Leibnitz, Dr. Samuel Clarke, Cudworth, Dr. Richard Fiddes, Rev. Colin Campbell, Mr. Wollaston, Moses Lowman, Dean Hamilton, Chevalier Ramsey, Mr. W. H. Gillespie, and others. Of that of Mr. Gillespie, entitled *The Necessary Existence of God*, Sir William Hamilton says: "I consider it among the very best specimens of speculative philosophy which this country has latterly exhibited." But it is too elaborate to be condensed For insertion here.

7. It only remains, now, to indicate, if possible, the right import and real force of the ontological proof as it has been thus successively developed, and stands accredited in present thought. This involves the following points:

First, in most of the forms in which it usually appears, notably the older forms, such as Anselm's, Descartes', and others shaped in their method, it certainly failed to be a demonstration. It is seriously faulty and inconclusive. It confounds conceptual existence, and existence *in re*. In the curious and delusive legerdemain of thought and word involved in it, the reasoning makes it seem as if the interval between subjective idea and real being had been successfully crossed, and that, at least in this case, what is ideal in the mind must be real beyond the mind. But this is an illusion, under the shadow of the moving and changing phrases. It fails to show that the simple fact of our conceiving of a being, whether contingent or necessary being, imperfect or perfect, is positive proof of the objective existence of such being. Our conceiving of a being is one thing, the real existence of that being is quite another. No matter if the conception of God is unique and peculiar, as is claimed, and, unlike the conception of contingent beings, involves *necessity* of existence, it is still only a conception. The argument puts the simple *conception* of a "necessary existence" as equivalent to the proof of the necessity of that existence. The manipulation, however, fails to make sure the objective reality by a mere contingent thought within us.

Secondly, although defective, this evidence, even in its Anselmic and Cartesian form, is by no means valueless. The ideas with whose presence in the mind it deals, and whose implications it seeks to solve, form the basis of reasoning of great theistic force. It supplies a leading element for a proof in calling attention to the point that the true idea of God is that of a Being "necessarily existent." To think Him truly, at all, we must think Him as existing. Existence is a necessary element in the *idea* of God. In this fundamental principle there is firm ground; God is not thought truly unless He is thought as a *necessarily existent* being. But the lack here appears. For though he cannot be truly thought as a contingent Being, the question may still be raised, whether it is necessary to think the thought of God at all. The thought itself may possibly be contingent, a mere product of our free ability to make it or not. The argument is fatally defective unless it can be shown that this *idea* is a *necessary* one.

Thirdly, this question, whether the forming of the idea of God is contingent or necessary, upon which everything now depends, is answered by abundant evidence showing that it is *necessary*. It is not an arbitrary product, like the fictions which the imagination has power to make or not, at pleasure, but it is inevitable in the normal action of the reason, and indispensable to every rational consideration of things. Kant and others have thoroughly established the truth that this idea necessarily arises in the mind when developed and exercised in contact with the phenomena of the world and the experiences of life. From our knowledge of extended material objects, and of occurring events, and states of consciousness, the ideas of Space and Time are necessarily developed. In somewhat similar way, in presence of the facts of the universe and our mental experiences, through our knowledge of limited, dependent, and begun existences, the ideas of Cause, Infinity, Independence, and Self-existence are inevitably evoked. The infinite and the absolute are required as correlates of the finite and contingent, and seen to be as real as are the contingent realities of actual experience which call for them. It does not matter that these ideas are conditioned in the elements of experience. So are the necessary notions of Time, Space, and Cause. Yet these notions are so fundamental and necessary that thinking is impossible without them. Even the contingent, but actual, realities of the world cannot be thought at all without involving them. Nor does it matter that no one of these ideas is in itself the full concept or idea of God. For in their union and implications they necessarily amount to that idea, as well as evoke it. With these necessary truths of Cause, the Infinite, the Absolute, or the Independent, or Self-existent, the idea of God as the infinite and self-existent Being spontaneously and by inexorable logic, completes itself. It has thus the validity of a necessary thought. The theistic conclusion is, therefore, well assured, under the principle that what the human mind must *necessarily think*, and must think as *necessarily existing*, cannot be doubted. We add the argument as condensed and shaped by Dr. Dorner:

"1. When the highest essence is thought, it is thought as unconditioned and independent of anything else; independent, also, of our subjective thought, but as unconditioned or absolute, self-existent. Thus the only *choice* lies between leaving the idea of God unthought, or thinking it, when thought, absolute and self-existing.

"2. But this double possibility does not hold, and thus the hypothetical alternative is rather established. It is not optional, but necessary to think an Absolute, which, in order to be thought, is to be thought as existent. It is necessary, that is to say, for him who wishes to think rationally, and whose thought *is* thought which would become knowledge.... It is not open to the rational thinker to avow an Absolute—he *must* avow it."

The points in the argument may, therefore, be summed up thus:

First, the rational idea of being is not a mere abstraction, an optional product of our own faculties. We know *real* being by *intuition*.

Secondly, we necessarily have an idea of real being.

Thirdly, but contingent and dependent being does not fill out the idea of real being, and we are compelled to think of *ultimate* being, involving the ideas of self-existence, independence, and eternity. Thus by a single analysis of our necessary idea and knowledge of real being, we find it to include an Absolute or Self-existent Being. The ontological argument is simply an analysis of the first great fact of our consciousness—the consciousness of existence. If we believe in existence at all, as we must, we must believe in an Eternal Existence, Absolute Existence. In so far as this Absolute Existence is necessarily identical with God, the evidence is conclusive.

Fourthly, the only way of evading the force of this evidence as now fully constructed under the philosophy of necessary truths, is by undermining, if possible, the validity of these necessary ideas. This is attempted. Kant himself prepared the way for this. Though he showed so clearly the necessity of the notions of Time, Space, Cause, God, he yet questioned whether they were anything more than forms of thought, necessary and regulative indeed for us, but not certainly pointing to objective realities. Though universal and inevitable, they are viewed as purely subjective, only forms of sensible consciousness, with no certain validity for "things in themselves," or real being. In this doubt as to the reliability of our necessary knowledge, or its validity for the real world, Kant has been followed by many. It underlies and marks the whole philosophy of agnosticism, if indeed agnosticism can have a philosophy. It is not in place here to repeat the many all-sufficient answers to this negative part of the Kantian doctrine. It is purely dogmatic, and not required by anything demonstrated in the positive nature of the necessary rational perceptions. It is in utter contradiction to the whole science of knowledge.

Fifthly, it is thus apparent that whether the ontological evidence be accepted as a demonstration or not, it is of very great legitimate force. For the only alternative to admitting it is to discredit the *a priori* judgments and trustworthiness of reason. What more can be asked for, in a proof, than that it should present a logical conclusion which cannot be set aside without assuming that the human mind in its ultimate principles is self-contradictory and deceptive? Probably the words of Prof. Flint are not too strong to sum up the results from this argument: "This, it may be objected, is not equivalent to a proof of the existence of an infinite and eternal Being. It leads merely to the alternative, either that infinite and eternal Being exists, or that the consciousness and reason of man cannot be trusted. The absolute skeptic will rejoice to have this alternative offered to him; that the human mind is essentially untrustworthy is precisely what he maintains. I answer that I admit the arguments in question do not amount to a direct proof, but they constitute a *reductio ad absurdum*, which is just as good, and that if they do not exclude absolute skepticism, it is merely because absolute skepticism is willing to accept what is absurd.... If though I am constrained to conclude that there is an infinite and eternal Being, I may reject the conclusion on the supposition that reason is untrustworthy, I am clearly bound, in self-consistency, to set aside the testimony of my senses also by the assumption that they are habitually delusive. When any view or theory is shown to involve absolute skepticism, it is sufficiently refuted; for absolute skepticism effaces the distinction between reason and unreason, and practically prefers unreason to reason."

It is proper, at this place, to exclude and disown some forms of alleged proof sometimes put forward as *a priori* or closely allied to it. Whatever evidence may lie in germ or by implication in the facts they present, they cannot be accepted when offered as complete proofs. It is difficult to understand how they should ever be given as such. Probably those who exalt them most would never have brought them forward had they not first allowed bewildering speculative difficulties to break their hold of the real and best theistic evidences. In their doubt of the true, they have clutched at the false.

The first is the claim that the soul is *immediately conscious* of God. German writers have been fond of this representation. But to assert such a direct "God-consciousness" (*Gottes-bewusstsein*) is either to use the term "consciousness" with a strange and misleading meaning, or to declare as a fact what is without evidence and incapable of proof. Psychology shows us, indeed, that the consciousness may include objective realities, in certain ways and to some degree. Some *non-ego* is a co-agent in giving existence to every mental state. But this is through the sense-perceptions. Through these we may say we are conscious of external objects. For in the act of perception our consciousness properly includes three objects, viz.: the mental act or state, the ego acting, and the outer object which determines the act. We may, in a sense, therefore, speak of being conscious of the material world about us and of our fellow-men. But this knowledge of external objects is more properly credited to sense-perception consciously exercised. Moreover, with respect to knowing God, this only perceptive faculty for external or non-egoistic objects falls utterly short; for no one will claim that God is an object of sense-perception. If, however, it should be said that we are directly conscious of the supersensible realities of time, cause, power, etc., it is enough to reply that we are conscious of them simply *as* time, cause, and power, and that the idea and proof of God are developed from these, even in the ontological way, only by a more or less extended logical process. We know of no mode in which the consciousness can directly inform us of more than what is wholly subjective, except through the action of the sense-perceptions and the processes of thought. Writers who resolve the theistic proof into an immediate consciousness of God are dealing in a mysticism that disregards clear thinking, and avoids the very explanation needed—how a knowledge of God is given *to* consciousness. Of course, when we once know God, through any mode by which our intellect may apprehend His existence, we are then conscious of knowing Him. This, however, is a direct *consciousness* only of our own intellectual state.

The second is the assertion of an *immediate intuition* of God. However evident the divine existence may become under proper showing, it is not self-evident. It is not a truth seen to be clear in the simple terms of its statement. Even the ontological argument does not claim that it is so. Else no argument would be used—none would be needed. If men stood face to face with God, perceiving Him directly in immediate vision, the whole history of this effort to establish the divine existence to the reason would be inexplicable. There are, indeed, various *a priori* elements involved in the apprehension of God, such as the intuitions of Time, Space, Causality, Infinity, Self-existence; but these alone, and simply *as* intuitions, are neither the concept of God nor the existence of God. They are simply the materials out of which, in connection with our knowledge of the facts of external nature, the judgments of the reason may show the existence of God to be necessary. A mixture of both intuitional and experiential elements is involved. The very idea of God is built up cumulatively, and the affirmation, "God exists," stands only as the authorized conclusion from the premises.

A *third* notion to be thrown out is that man has an *immediate feeling* of God. Though the absurdity of this notion makes it unworthy of notice, the frequent repetition of it makes a notice necessary. Psychology makes no truth plainer than that feeling or emotion, *i.e.*, the action of the mental sensibilities, depends and waits on knowing, and that a man feels, or can feel, only in so far as he perceives or knows something that excites feeling. Simple feeling, without knowing, is a purely imaginary and really impossible experience. To put it in front as a direct apprehension of God only illustrates the nonsense which good men sometimes substitute for legitimate evidence.

With equal emphasis we must reject another form of representation, that the divine existence is wholly a matter of *faith*, faith as distinguished from knowledge and instead of it. Led by false metaphysics, some writers have conceded that God cannot be *known* by the finite mind. Some of them yet claim that we must believe in Him. Holding that His existence lies wholly beyond the reach of our knowledge, that we can know neither *that* He is nor *what* He is, they assert that we can and ought to apprehend Him by faith. Though this view is endorsed by great names, it is, so far as Natural Theology is concerned, utterly misleading. For unless the word is used in a strangely private and inapplicable sense, the claim entirely misconceives the true relation between knowledge and faith. A mere belief, without a reason or knowledge to justify it, is arbitrary, and rests on nothing. Faith must always rest on or in knowledge. It demands some evidence to justify it. This evidence must precede, to beget faith. Belief dies out if not supported and justified by reason. If it rests only on and in itself, if it has no warrant but the very act of believing, and is not implied by real knowledge, it is irrational and without authority. In the sphere of Natural Theology, therefore, where by definition we are not believing in the divine existence on the testimony of revelation, mere faith can furnish no just ground for the theistic conclusion.

Into this baseless position all agnostic theories seek to put the great truth of theism. In placing it wholly beyond the sphere of the knowable they allow it to stand, if it is to stand at all, in the confidence of men only through an inexplicable and arbitrary act of faith as a necessity of the feelings. But there is no need of consenting to this non-rational character of the basis of theism. There is no wisdom in doing so. The true vindication of theism is not reached by such compromising consent to the demands of an untenable and spurious philosophy, but by showing that the faith in this great truth is a faith justly evoked by knowledge, and authorized by invincible intellectual data.

Natural Theology

CHAPTER III

THE COSMOLOGICAL EVIDENCE

THE special evidence designated by this term is drawn from a consideration of the world in the particular aspects of *contingency, finiteness*, and *dependence*. Instead of dealing simply with the primary and necessary ideas of the mind, as the ontological method professes to do, this gives attention specially to the existence of the external world, and draws its evidence from it. In thus considering the world, however, it does not concern itself with either the special or general indications of purpose or design in the order and structure of nature, but deals with its phenomena simply as exhibiting a system of originated, limited, and dependent being. It is the intention of this chapter to present in brief, first the substance of this argument, and then the value and amount of its legitimate conclusion.

There are two fundamental and essential parts in the argument. The first is the *a priori principle and law of causation*. The second is that *the world, whether viewed in its parts or as a whole, is a finite and dependent existence*. These two things must be examined separately.

1. In accepting and proceeding upon the principle expressed in the law of causation: "*Every event, or contingent phenomenon, must have a cause*" it rests on a self-evident and necessary judgment of the human mind. It is one of those "first truths" which shine in their own light, with full certainty and absolute authority. It is not simply evident, it is self-evident. It is intuitively seen to be a necessary truth, as soon as its terms are

understood. Its contradictory is inconceivable. Efforts have indeed been steadily made to bring its validity into doubt—such as the assertion that it may be only a "form of thought," subjectively unavoidable, but without authority for real being; or that it results as a simple appearance from the "impotence of the mind "to think beyond experience; or that it expresses only an empirical "order of succession," a mere time-relation of habitually observed antecedence and sequence, no real power or efficiency being involved. And this makes it proper, by a brief examination of the law, to assure ourselves of its validity.

(1) The primary idea of cause arises out of our consciousness and experience. Every man directly knows himself as a cause—of thoughts, volitions, and actions. He finds causes, also, in the outer world. He is compelled, by both consciousness and experience, to hold them as real—real for his own activities, real for nature. This simply accounts for the origin of the idea. It begins in particular instances of real causation.

(2) A cause, properly defined, is that by which anything that was not comes to be. It means the power that produces a change or event. The essence of the idea is that of activity, or an efficient energy in genuine relation to a result. "The connection between cause and effect is nothing more or less than the connection between action and its result. This connection is of the nature of a necessity; it partakes of the necessities of thought itself." A cause, therefore, is not simply something that precedes an event, but something that, while preceding, is *effective* for it. This at once answers and excludes the notion which makes the law but an expression of a time-relation.

(3) The *law* of causation, formally expressed, is that "every event must have a cause." It affirms this dependence of "events," *i.e.*, any begun existences, or changes, or phenomena, upon causes, as universal. It does not say every "effect," for then the proposition would involve only the self-evidence of verbal correlatives. But it is impossible to conceive of something arising absolutely or uncaused out of nothing. *Ex nihilo nihil fit.* The human mind is compelled to hold all "events," or whatever was not but begins to be, *as* effects.

(4) This law of causation is *intuitively* perceived to be certain and universal. It bears the tests of self-evidence, necessity, and universality.

(5) Its valid authority is further supported by the fact that its truth is necessarily and actually assumed as fundamental in all the processes of knowledge, in all the activities of life, in all reasoning, whether inductive or deductive. It is assumed as a precondition to the very inductions which are sometimes claimed to give the law.

(6) If it be said that the apparent necessary universality of the law is due simply to our uniform experience only of *caused* events, and an incompetency to transcend experience, and that with a different experience we might conceive of them without any cause whatever, it is enough to reply that this is at best only an *unknown* possibility. And this suggestion of "mental impotence" presenting only a negative, an *inability* to think the contradictory of the law, has no right to annul a *positive* affirmation of thought. For the causal judgment gives us the positive side—an affirmative judgment, that stands authorized in its own light, no matter what impotence of thought may be surmised.

But even if the causal judgment should be conceded to rest on a one-sided, though uniform, experience of mankind, its practical validity would be scarcely less than if viewed as a pure intuition. For that the experience of the race, in its millions on millions and through all ages, has found no events without causes, so as to lift thinking out of this impotency, ought to be sufficient to prove what is the actual truth of things, and to accredit the causal law as trustworthy.

(7) These same principles apply to the Kantian doubt whether the form of thought is entitled to hold for objective reality. Kant has derived the idea of cause from sensible consciousness of events in time, and makes the law of causality, considered as a principle of physical science, purely a law of "order in time," and not a power or efficiency. It denotes simply the fact of regular phenomenal sequence. His view of it is part of a system of relativity of knowledge or phenomenalism which so thoroughly separates the world, as apprehended under the modifying,

coloring, and creative action of our perceiving faculties, from the world as it is in itself, or in reality, that our knowledge becomes unreliable for its interpretation. The laws of its real existence, it represents, are beyond our knowledge; we have only mentally imposed appearances, which are unable to carry us to the real truth of things. This error has been often and ably pointed out, but the elaborate refutations cannot be rehearsed here. Several points will suffice. First, that Kant has, in finding the idea of cause essentially in temporal antecedence and sequence, really given a spurious concept of it. And, secondly, in questioning its validity for real existence while asserting its intuitive necessity as a "form of knowledge," he discredits the trustworthiness of the human faculties for the ascertainment of truth. The method of *reductio ad absurdum* is applicable here. This imputation of illusion and falseness to our necessary forms of thought is intellectual suicide. If that which is most clear, most universal, and most permanent in both sensuous and rational perception, and is of necessity "regulative "for every kind of knowledge, both common and scientific, is, after all, only a mental fiction, a ghostly shadow, then the whole superstructure of knowledge floats away in air. To deny such primitive truths is to remove the foundations of all knowledge and fall into absolute skepticism. If this overthrows the proofs of theism, it at the same time overthrows the arguments against theism. These consequences do not, indeed, prove the validity of the law of causation, but they show the impossibility of disproof of it. The law remains unaffected by the theory that questions it, because the theory annihilates itself in the self-destroying force and absurdity of its own implications.

(8) But the method of science makes a vindication of the validity of the law of causation hardly needful in our day. This has refused to recognize, or be disturbed by, these discrediting suggestions. So far as metaphysics keeps on questioning its validity, it is out of harmony with the great working principle of science. The reality and universality of the law of causation is the grand fundamental postulate of all scientific investigation and conclusions. It is assumed and believed without a doubt. It is followed with a confidence that is impatient of any question as to

the safety of the conclusions which it authorizes. The great working idea of the science of the age is that all nature is moving and developing under invariable causal law, that all phenomena are capable of explanation by being brought under the connections it expresses, and that by the guidance of this law of cause and effect it may trace back the line and order of the earth's evolution, and write out the story of its development, from the earliest geologic and astronomic beginnings. Never before did science, with such unhesitating belief, make this self-evident law of causation its working principle in endeavor to find the beginnings and understand the realities of nature. It takes it as absolutely universal, necessary, and valid for all contingent phenomena and truth, practically dismissing speculative difficulties as of no account.

The first part of this cosmological evidence is, therefore, one of the deepest and most incontestable principles or laws known to the human mind: "Everything that has a beginning must have a cause—an adequate cause." That is to say, only self-existent, eternally existent being can be without a cause.

2. The other part is: *The universe, whether viewed in its parts or as a whole*, is necessarily *viewed as a finite and dependent existence*. This includes several affirmations:

First, the *real existence* of the universe. It may seem superfluous to assert so plain a truth, but nothing is superfluous which helps to obviate doubts and insure certainty in this reasoning. We obtain a clear and certain starting point in our immediate and necessary consciousness of *self* as existing. No man can doubt his own existence. In thinking, feeling, acting, he finds himself, in an immediate knowledge. In his sensible consciousness he also necessarily apprehends something not self. This not-self, or external something, also is directly and unavoidably known.

On both the subjective and objective sides, therefore, real existence is assured, whatever account may be given of the reality. And when through sensible experience, under the guidance and completing help of the reason, we obtain the widest and most thorough knowledge that scientific research can give of the great universe, we know it, with valid certainty, as really existing.

Secondly, this universe is *finite and dependent*, and cannot, therefore, have the ultimate reason or ground of its existence in itself. Nature, not only in all its parts without exception, but as unified under the completest generalizations of science, is found to be limited, finite, and dependent. Everything is conditioned in and on something else, and this in turn on others. Everything is made what it is by existing in relation to other things. This is true of all the existences and phenomena that constitute a world, and of systems of worlds. Independent, non-conditioned existence is discovered nowhere. In the organic world the dependence and limitation are conspicuous. Every mind is limited in power. The entire assemblage of existences and phenomena known or conceived of in space and time, is an aggregate of parts dependent on parts equally dependent. No addition of finite existences can make an infinite. No accumulation of dependent existences can make the independent. The whole, therefore, forms a finite and dependent universe. The cause of it, therefore, cannot be found in itself. If we run back through the connections of its existences and phenomena, we find only causes which are in themselves effects requiring preceding causes. An "infinite series" of dependent existences is a contradiction in terms and impossible in thought. A chain of dependent things cannot hang on nothing. There must be a first cause for it. Hence for this finite and dependent universe, as a *whole*, there must be a self-existent and independent cause. An infinite, unconditioned, *i.e.*, independent, cause is the necessary correlate to a finite and conditioned universe.

3. There are two ways in which this conclusion has been supposed to be brought into doubt. One is by denying that our necessary laws of thought—in this case the law of causation—are applicable to the real universe, and the other by claiming that the universe itself may be infinite and eternal. A brief explanation, however, will show how little reason there is for doubt from either of these points.

(1) The only ground on which it is said that the law of causation cannot be taken as holding in this relation, is the

suggestion that all our knowledge of the world is a factitious product of our sensible consciousness, and that of things as they really are, or "in themselves," we know nothing. The theory teaches a "relativity "which leaves all knowledge a pure phenomenalism, and puts an impassable gulf between all appearances and the possible realities. It "arbitrarily assumes that there is no correspondence between things as they really are and things as they *appear to us*." It questions whether our subjective law of thought is also a law of things. But it *concedes* that if things really are as they are apprehended, the law *is* both valid and necessarily applicable. And it must be remembered that this supposition that things in themselves are different from the forms in which our minds must know them, is wholly gratuitous and without warrant. "The same incompetency of our faculties which prevents us from asserting that things really are as they appear to us, equally forbids us to maintain that they are *not* as they appear." We surely have no warrant to say that they are *not* as we *know them to be by all our faculties* of knowing. And more than this—if any principle has been adequately and firmly settled in the progress of philosophy, it is that real "being "is the only true reason and explanation of "knowing." The *ratio cognoscendi* is founded on the *ratio essendi*. All knowledge begins, through both sense-perception and consciousness, in a knowledge of *being*—ourselves and realities around us. Even space as the condition for material bodies, comes out of our knowledge of body in the concrete, with three dimensions. So time, as the condition for events, is known through a conscious succession of individual existences, both mental and physical. All true knowledge, at its very roots, is ontological, or knowledge of real being. The theory of the pure subjectivity of Time, Space, Cause, etc., is utterly contradicted by the fundamental process of knowing. Space is known as a form of things before it is known as a form of thought. Time in the realities of actual duration is known before the generic concept of Time. Cause is known as a real power before it is generalized as a law. Our knowing is guided by being. The philosophy that abandons this principle can be no guide whatever to the truth of things.

(2) The suggestion that the universe itself may be infinite and eternal is without supporting evidence. It is not only opposed to the natural appearance of things, but disowned by some of the most thoroughly assured conclusions of science. In the face of these the oft-repeated supposition of "an eternal succession," in its customary or accredited sense, has no place. Science admits not only each man to have had a beginning, but the race itself, animal life and organizations of all sorts, the rocks of the globe, the very globe itself, the whole solar system, and systems of systems. It postulates a time when the earth was not. Science, as well as theology, has turned its efforts to account for the "genesis" of the world. And the accepted, if not established, theories of modern science have failed to find infinity or eternity in the physical universe. Its fundamental working basis is the postulate of *atoms*, as the ultimate particles or units by whose juxtaposition the chemical substances and the whole world of bodies, with all their forms, states, and changes, are composed or produced. Atoms are used as the necessary presuppositions to explain the genesis and occurrence of all the phenomena which constitute the universe of known existence. This is the atomo-mechanical theory, now dominating scientific work. These hypothetical atoms are variously conceived of; by some as ultimate units with actual extension, hard and inelastic, by others as perfectly elastic. Some consider them not as material elements, but centers of force. Some conceive "energy" as disparate, and speak of matter *and* force, others as inherent and one with the atoms. Still others hold the atoms to be vortex-rings or motions in a homogeneous and perfectly frictionless fluid existing in space. The conception under which the atomic theory may be summarized and unified is that the atom is an ultimate particle or point in which a series of motions manifest themselves. It is of course impossible to conceive of motion without anything to move, or without force or energy acting in relation to the particle or point moving. According to the atomo-mechanical theory, therefore, atoms and motion lie at the origin and development of the physical universe. Thus matter, and all phenomenal being as known by human sense-perception, are resolved into "modes of motion." All forces are considered as one and the same force

differently manifested in these modes of motion. The "conservation" or "persistence of energy," and its "correlation" or transfer from form to form and from potential to active state and back again without loss, follows as a part of the mechanical explanation. The idea is given that the sum total of matter and energy in the universe is constant, none being added, none destroyed. It is always either manifested as force or becomes potential, though quiet, as power.

Now it is true that this theory, viewed in the gross, has been used to give color to the notion that the universe may have been in motion from eternity and will continue to eternity, that it is not dependent, but infinite in time, a self-existent perpetual motion. But a closer examination shows this conclusion to be hasty and unauthorized. When we reach the teleological argument, with its great facts of order, adjustment, and specific organizations, the impotence of the theory in itself to account for the universe as we find it will become fully evident. It is only necessary here to point out that it fails to prove that the universe is not finite and dependent. (*a*) The atoms being finite particles or centers of force, the supposition of an infinitely extended universe can be gotten only by assuming the atoms to be infinite in number. But even this is inadequate; for no addition of finites can give the true infinite. Here a fact of limitation at once enters—limitation in extension. (*b*) A probable limitation in time also appears. The "conservation of energy" is found to be qualified by the counter truth of the "dissipation of energy." The transformations have not been found absolutely complete or the movements always fully reversible. Under tests mathematically applied, in some relations mechanical energy has shown a tendency to become more and more dissipated. Matter not under the control of organic life exhibits a tendency toward a stable equilibrium. Attention has often been called to this, in its relation to the astronomical systems. The sun is radiating into space an enormous amount of energy, as light and heat. The supply, though it may last for many millions of years, is not inexhaustible. Some of the heat is received by surrounding planets, but much of it must pass out beyond the limits of the universe as known to us, radiated in every direction into space.

Science, though it has labored at the problem, knows no way in which it can be restored. The sun is cooling, the planets are cooling, the stream of chief energy for the whole system is diminishing. In the words of Clausius, who has called special attention to this fact: "If transformations in one definite direction exceed in magnitude those in the opposite direction, the entire condition of the universe must always continue to change in that first direction, and the universe must consequently approach incessantly to a limiting condition." This dissipation tends to final equilibrium, and this, under the mechanical theory that all things are modes of motion, is undistinguishable from annihilation. (*c*) The only conceivable way of avoiding this conclusion is by supposing the number of bodies in the universe to be really infinite. Then the radiation would all be re-absorbed. The energy would all be retained within it somewhere. A re-transformation could be conceived as occurring in great cycles, and the universe might be eternal. But not only does this supposition offer a purely imaginary hypothesis, but it impales itself on the fact that an infinite number of worlds is impossible from the finite atoms with which the theory starts. Limitation is an essential quality of matter, whether as atoms or aggregations of them. No multiplication of it can yield an infinite universe. The universe is thus limited in both space and time, even when viewed in the light of the mechanical theory. The conclusion, therefore, remains substantially unimpaired: For this finite and conditioned universe there must be a self-existent, unconditioned, eternal cause. (*d*) Another fact of limitation must be included. In *mind* we have a succession of distinct personal beings, begun in time, non-material entities, limited in number and power. These are to be added to the aggregate of physical nature, to make up the universe as we know it. Neither science nor philosophy has as yet succeeded in identifying matter and mind, or establishing the theory of monism or the existence of only one substance or kind of being. We may safely affirm that it cannot do it. For monism necessarily breaks at the start by arbitrarily denying the veracity of consciousness, which immediately and necessarily presents a knowledge of both the ego and the non-ego in irreducible antithesis. This ego or self is the only strictly individual and indivisible being that we know—lying in the deepest foundation of all our knowledge. The reasoning that attempts to count out self-conscious mind from real being, by refuting consciousness, refutes itself in pushing all knowledge from its primary and only basis. Here, then, in human minds, is a world of self-conscious, self-determining, spiritual, or at least non-material dependent beings, for which a cause is needed. Science confesses that it has no solution for living, free, self-conscious beings, in any known qualities or powers of matter. This fact adds force to the demand for the existence of an infinite, unconditioned First Cause. Indeed, it requires a self-conscious First Cause.

4. It is to be conceded that the cosmological proof lacks in direct force for the establishment of the *personality* of the self-existent First Cause. In itself, as usually stated, or without including the fact and presence of *mind* in the world, the argument might be held to prove only a self-existent *something*, perhaps an impersonal, blind force or energy, without the attributes which necessarily enter into the conception of God. We need further and different evidences, to secure us against the Scylla and Charybdis of materialism and pantheism. However, without as yet drawing upon teleology, this argument, when its implications are developed, goes far toward the proof of personality. For (1) by necessary conception a First Cause is one, not many; (2) the First Cause must be a *free* Cause; for that which is first is truly unconditioned, self-existent, and self-determining; (3) a Free Cause must be an *intelligent* Cause. We never reach the sphere of freedom until we emerge from the material into the spiritual, until we leave matter and reach mind. By consent of all great thinkers, self-determining being, being containing in itself the cause of its own activity and changes, is necessarily conceived of as Mind or intelligent Will. A self-determining personal Spirit or Mind, and intelligent Will alone, therefore, must be the First or Originating Cause. Logical necessity thus drives us, not only to assert the existence of an ultimate, independent Cause, but to regard that Cause as an Infinite Personality.

CHAPTER IV

THE TELEOLOGICAL EVIDENCE

FROM the earliest days of Greek philosophy men have been accustomed to vindicate their belief in an intelligent and wise author of the world by appealing to the evident marks of order, plan, and purpose in nature. Socrates pointed his disciples to numerous facts of clear adaptation and design as justifying his conclusion that "man must be the masterpiece of some great artificer," and that the stupendous universe "could not have been produced by chance, but by intelligence." The mind of Cicero was greatly impressed by these facts, and in his *De Natura Deorum* he employed them with much fullness and beauty of illustration. This way of reasoning has always been by far the most common method of theistic proof. This is not only because the materials it employs are open to the view of all men in even ordinary observation, and are strongly impressive, but because of the strength and certainty of the foundations on which it rests. The perpetual wonders of nature give it a perennial force. It is the most effective and useful form of proof, because it appeals to principles which a child can understand, and which a philosopher cannot explain away. It has not, indeed, been allowed to stand unchallenged. As might be expected, it has been subjected to the severest criticism. But though often assailed, it not only abides in the spontaneous reasoning of the human soul when face to face with nature, but it vindicates its metaphysical and logical soundness in the judgment of the profoundest and best balanced thought of our age. While materialists and atheists, apparently irritated by its evident force and influence, have invoked all possible resources of speculation against it, and even some theists, misled by specious but factitious difficulties or hasty timidity, have been betrayed into ill-advised and unnecessary concessions, the thorough discussions which have been called forth, in a measure that has given the subject a literature of exceeding richness, have but served to show its immovable foundations, and to buttress every essential part of the argument. When, as the outcome of a century of such discussion, the best assured results or conclusions of modern science and philosophy are summed up—as they have been summed up lately with clear discrimination and judicial calmness—the argument remains essentially unimpeached. We believe it is unimpeachable.

The teleological evidence—from τέλος, end, and λόγος, discourse or discussion—is derived from the manifold facts of order, purpose, design, or adaptation of means to ends, in nature. It reasons from the clear indications of plan, counsel, and thought in the economy of nature to the existence of a Thinker who stands to it in the relation of an intelligent Cause. While the cosmological argument rests upon the *contingency* of the world, this emphasizes the facts of order and aim, plan and adjustment, almost everywhere perceived. It is commonly called the argument from *final causes* or *design.* The term "final cause" was originated by the scholastics on the basis of Aristotle's fourfold distinction of causes. Giving Latin expression to Aristotle's phrases, they enumerated what we translate as the *"material cause"* the material elements; the *"formal cause"* the properties which constitute the form; the *"efficient cause"* the producing energy, and the *"final cause"* the end (*finis,* τέλος) on account of which, or for the sake of which (τὸ οὗ ἕνεκα), the action is done or the thing made. The teleological argument is, therefore, the application of the principle of "ends," "final causes," or design to the question of the being of God.

The aim of this chapter is to exhibit this form of evidence, as it stands in the light of present knowledge. Necessary brevity will restrict us, however, to the leading and essential parts of the proof. We divide the whole discussion into three sections, presenting successively a statement of the fundamental and general principles of the argument, the evidence of final cause in nature, and the valid necessity of concluding to the existence of an intelligent and self-determining cause that is God.

Natural Theology

SECTION I

EXPLANATIONS AND FUNDAMENTAL PRINCIPLES

1. *Definition of "final cause" or "design."* By a final cause is meant an *end (finis, τέλος) as predetermined and arranged for in the action of the forces which effect it.* It is illustrated whenever a movement or complex of movements is controlled or directed with a view to a specific and predetermined result. As the notion of final cause is primarily derived from consciousness, it will be best understood by looking at it in examples of human activity and experience. Take a common instance: A man makes a table. The immediate cause of the table is the mechanical action of the tools or work which shapes and combines the parts; but the determining cause is the intelligent purpose of the artisan. The effect, which appears at the close of the work, is, from the first, as an *idea*, the directing cause of the whole process. A table appears at the end only because a table is predetermined at the beginning. The end conceived and willed becomes the reason and explanation of what is done. The design becomes the real cause. Such an example gives us the fundamental conception of final cause. It shows that under it efficient causes become subordinate, being controlled and directed by the predetermined result. It involves three distinct conditions: (1) Foresight of an end; (2) determination to realize it; and (3) directive supremacy over all the forces by which as means the end is attained. As a complete definition, therefore, we may say that final cause is the purpose which, having conceived or idealized the end, coordinates and controls the whole series of phenomena of which that end

appears as the result. The end works as a design or purposive cause from the beginning.

The distinguishing characteristic, therefore, of final cause is *"adaptation to the future"* or *"coördination of means to specific ends."* And this explains the peculiar meaning of the word "design" when applied to this relation in nature. Exception has often been taken to its use in this argument. We are told that it is absurd to speak of design in unconscious nature, since the word expresses a function or act of the mind. It is true that subjectively and in primary sense design can exist only in mind. And the teleological argument not only recognizes this fact, but insists on it, and rests its final conclusion on it. But objectively and in secondary sense the term is properly applied to the adaptation, adjustment, order, arrangement, or mechanism which comes as the result or product of the action of a purposing intelligence. The human purpose, for instance, which conceived and made the watch to measure time, is recorded in the whole structure of the watch. The design, which started as an ideal, passes over into material structure as coordination and adaptation in the product. The watch is the maker's thought expressed and recorded. So we justly speak of design in the product—the adjustment of its parts to its intended use. In this secondary sense the word is rightly applied to the phenomena of nature, considered as exhibiting adaptations which have been determined by their intended ends. In this use of it nature is viewed as a visual language. Its phenomena are the visual words in which the human intelligence reads the thought, intention, or mind of its author. That the order, harmony, and adaptation which we discover in nature are actually and certainly due to a designing intelligence, as an engine is due to the human purpose which constructed it, is not, indeed, at this stage of the argument positively assumed. Such, however, is the clear and admitted appearance; and while the argument does not begin by at once assuming this conclusion, it proposes to investigate this unquestionable appearance, with full confidence that in the end these indications of thought and adaptation that crowd upon our view in nature will be seen to be invincible proofs of the existence and work of a thinker as the author of the world.

This general account of final cause fixes the meaning of a number of terms used in connection with it. (1) *Design*, when used objectively, stands for the end or adaptation as preconceived and accomplished by the designer. (2) *Adaptation* signifies the fitness of one thing to another. It may be the fitness of efficient causes to produce the intended result, of part to part in the structure of an organism, or of the whole organism to its purpose. (3) *Order* means regularity in coexistence or succession of events. It may be simply the uniformity which appears when the same causes, operating in the same circumstances, produce the same effects. It is not necessarily the result of intentionality. Or it may be "the intelligent arrangement of means to accomplish an end, the harmonious relation established between the parts for the good of the whole." In the former sense it implies only efficient causation; in the latter sense it involves final cause. Order alone, therefore, is not necessarily in all cases the proof of design.

2. *The relation of final to efficient cause.* This argument recognizes the *union* of these two kinds of causes in nature. It does this, it is believed, by no doubtful right. For in the very source of the first discovery of both forms of causation, in the human consciousness, they are found coexistent and concurrent. We know ourselves unquestionably as both designing and acting, as exerting both final and efficient causation.

Like the cosmological proof, this proceeds upon the great fundamental *a priori* principle of causality—that every event must have a cause. And it reads this law in its fullest scope and universality. It accepts the reality and regular action of force in all its known modes and characteristics, whether mechanical, chemical, or vital. In this it proceeds on the common basis of all philosophic science. It looks on nature, therefore, in this respect, with no private eye, but in the universally accepted view of both common and scientific observation. It believes that efficient causes are found everywhere, and that all events are brought about by them. Its fundamental position is that there must be a cause for every phenomenon. And, true to the law in its deepest and fullest conception, it enlarges the comprehension of it so as to say distinctly that the cause must be *adequate* to all that appears in the effect. The nature of the cause must be such as to account for the whole product. For an effect which reveals no adaptation, the law might be satisfied with a fortuitous or blind force; but for one that exhibits a clear purpose or composite adjustments, it demands an intelligent cause. For a complex movement, with parts wisely coordinated and held steadily and unmistakably to a useful end, it requires a foreseeing and designing cause. For a thought and plan actualized and recorded in a distinct structure, organism, and function, as in the eye for sight, or the ear for hearing, it requires a Thinker as the only sufficient cause. This full scope of the principle, therefore, includes final cause, or design, in the aggregate causal action necessary for the rational explanation of the phenomena of nature. In other words, efficient and final causes act together. They imply each other. For it will be seen in the progress of this evidence that many things in nature are capable of explanation only by the co-action of intelligence or purpose with the physical forces that produce them.

The relation to each other, claimed for these two kinds of cause, *i.e.*, for energy and design, must be clearly settled at this point. For it has often been overlooked, or strangely misconceived. Sometimes the two principles have been treated as inconsistent and contradictory. They have been spoken of as if they excluded each other. But there could hardly be a more thorough misconception. They are not antagonistic. On the contrary, they seek and require each other. Final causes demand efficient causes for their accomplishment. Reciprocally, efficient causes appeal to final causes, or useful predetermined ends, for their rational justification. The working of forces is justified only by the ends they serve in the universe. Human experience, every day, makes the harmony of these two kinds of causes absolutely certain. They are constantly found acting together, as the special purpose of the designer guides the various forces which he employs—which in such relation take the character of *means*—to the predetermined end.

But the two hold distinct and different relations to the aggregate result, the one supplying the productive work, the other securing the intended order and adaptation in the product, the one furnishing the means, the other coordinating the means to the end. When a telescope, for instance, has been made, it is the result of both efficient and final cause. For it is a product, not only of the mechanical forces that wrought it, but of the design which, preconceiving the end from the beginning, controlled the constructive work to present at last an instrument for scanning the starry heavens. The discovery of efficient causes in nature is, therefore, no argument against final causes. At this point atheistic materialists have allowed themselves to be deluded. For they have assumed that in simply pointing out how the particular effects in any natural phenomenon result from some ascertained physical action, they have excluded final cause, or made it inapplicable. This has been well called a "most glaring example of the fallacy of irrelevant conclusion, or *ignoratio elenchi*." Design is not disproved in the watch by showing every movement of the tools and property of the metals with which it has been made. Every *end* requires *means, i.e.,* a cause fit to produce the effect. To discover this cause is in no way to destroy the idea of the end. It is, on the contrary, to exhibit the condition *sine qua non* for the production of the end. Nothing, therefore, is proved against final cause in nature when organic effects are traced to their proximate causes and determining conditions. We shall have frequent occasion to apply this truth in tracing this form of evidence.

3. *The alternative to final cause is chance.* This fact must be clearly distinguished and remembered. The point to be settled here is not whether really, or to an omniscient view, there is such a thing as chance in the world, but in what sense the word is to be understood when used in speaking of actual events. To say that a thing has come by chance is no denial of an efficient cause. It is viewed, not as without cause, but without design. It is not of chance simply by its cause being unknown. The cause of many events is inscrutable, but they are not regarded as fortuitous. But the term is applied to what has not been planned or intended. When a die is thrown the face presented comes as the result of sure laws of force and motion, but because not controlled by an intention it is said to be by chance. Should three letters, tossed on the floor, fall so as to spell, say the word "cup," the occurrence would be regarded as fortuitous, because unintended. There is in such cases a *coincidence* of efficient causes, moving

independently, issuing on a result not predetermined. Two travelers journeying to different points may meet where their ways cross. The meeting would take place by chance, *i.e.*, not without cause, but without design. This kind of coincidence is chance—a coincidence of causes in an event not foreseen or arranged. How incapable this very uncertain coincidence is to produce or preserve order and useful ends must not be forgotten when we come to scan the finely adjusted relations and wonderful organisms of nature.

4. *We view the validity of the principle of final cause as resting only on experience and induction.* Many able thinkers put it higher, and regard it as ranking with *a priori* self-evident and universal truths. President Porter, for example, has ably vindicated its right to be looked upon in this character: "We assert that the relation of means and ends is assumed *a priori* to be true of every event and being in the universe, and that the mind directs its inquiries by, and rests its knowledge upon, this as an intuitive principle." He shows how it is *presupposed* in the whole inductive process, and underlies all scientific thought and work, refusing to disappear from our conceptions of even those parts of nature where it seems utterly to hide itself. But this question is still under discussion, and serious difficulties are pointed out against this view. We are reminded of the fact that final cause has not actually and always asserted itself as self-evident, necessary, and universal, with the absolute resistlessness with which the law of causality does. No *law of thought* bars from limiting its application. Occurrences without design are not unthinkable. The idea of design is called forth, not with an absolute necessity, but only in the contemplation of particular features or parts of nature. If nature presented only physical or chemical facts, inorganic and general masses, an intelligence that should contemplate them would probably be satisfied by an explanation which would simply attach each phenomenon to its anterior cause, without ever raising the question of design. It seems to be dependent on the nature of the result whether a final cause is suggested to the observer or not. It is only because there are some phenomena which physical causes alone are incompetent to explain, that the addition of final cause becomes a necessity of

thought. But this at once limits the necessary evolution of the idea of design, and diminishes it from the necessity and universality of the law of efficient cause. In looking on the eruption of a volcano, or the irregular and confused outline and form of mountain chains and gaps, or the location of the fragments thrown by a dynamite discharge, we are compelled to think, if we think at all, that each result, however accidental it may seem, has had an adequate and specific efficient cause, but we are not equally obliged to believe that each has an intended end or purpose. "Take the eruption of a volcano," says Janet, "each stream of lava, each exhalation, each noise, each flash has its own cause, and the most passing of these phenomena could be determined *a priori* by him who knew accurately all the causes and all the conditions which brought about the eruption; but to think to attribute to each of these phenomena in particular a precise end is absolutely impossible. For what end is such a stone thrown to the right rather than the left? Why such an emanation rather than such another? These are questions which, in fact, no one asks. One might cite a thousand other examples: Why, to what end, do the clouds driven by the wind take such a form rather than such another? Why, to what end, does the malady called madness produce such a delusion rather than another? To what end has one monster two heads and another none at all? There are a thousand such cases, in which the human mind seeks causes without concerning itself about ends. I do not merely say that it ignores them, I say that it does not think of them, and is not forced to suppose them; while as to the causes, even when it is ignorant of them, it yet knows them to exist, and it believes in them invincibly.... If there are in the universe a great number of phenomena which do not suggest in any manner the idea of an end, to compensate for this there are others which, rightly or wrongly, call forth this idea imperiously and infallibly. Such are the organs of living beings, and above all, of the superior animals. Why this difference? What more is there in this case than in the previous one? If the principle of finality were universal and necessary, like the principle of causality, would we not apply it everywhere like the latter, and with the same certainty? There are none of these differences as regards efficient causes. In all cases we affirm that they exist, and we affirm it equally. There are no phenomena that are more evidently effects than others. We know the cause of them, or do not know it; but known or unknown, it is; and it is not more probable in this case than in that. On the other hand, even those who affirm that there is final cause everywhere, acknowledge that it is more manifested in the animal and vegetable kingdoms than in the mineral; and if one were reduced to the latter kingdom, and man were to forget himself, the idea of final cause would not, perhaps, present itself to the mind."

This account of the principle is not to be taken as any denial of the universal prevalence of final causation in nature. In the end we may believe in such a prevalence. When once, through analogy and induction, the principle has been recognized, and nature is read with the open eye of theistic vision, the conviction will probably come that the teleological law holds in all things throughout the universe. The completed induction may give to it such a certainty and necessity as to become regulative for the rational interpretation of all nature. We believe that nothing short of this will furnish a rational view or conception of the world, or justify the effort of science to set forth an orderly classification of its phenomena. This argument, however, does not assume final cause to be *a priori* or self-evident. It looks upon it simply as a reasoned truth, revealed in the facts of nature and thoroughly established by legitimate evidences.

5. The reasoning employed in this proof is *analogical and inductive*. It proceeds upon the indisputable fact of *likeness* between many of the products of nature and the products of human design. It is by no means claimed that they resemble each other in all respects. In many features they greatly differ. They are unlike as to the modes of production. Between the mechanism which produces a watch and the growth which produces a tree there is a complete difference. The difference is sometimes thought to destroy the ground of analogical reasoning in the case. The world, it has often been said, cannot be likened to Paley's watch or any other sort of mechanism. Between things natural and things which men make there are many most striking contrasts. But still, though the structures of nature are so

different from those of human art that they are at once easily distinguishable, and though the forces and processes by which they are formed bear no resemblance to each other, they have nevertheless something in common, and that common something is the evident adaptation to useful ends. This adaptation, too, is simply a *fact* in both cases. This is a point that must be clearly understood. We are to distinguish between the subjective design and the objective adaptation. The one is a mental act and force, the other a relation of parts in a product. Adaptation is not some ideal figment, formed somehow in our minds, and then arbitrarily transferred and imposed on nature, but is a perceived relation in and among objective and real phenomena. The adaptations in a chronometer are simply facts. The adaptations, likewise, in natural organisms, the suitableness of one part to the rest and of all to the uses of sentient existence, to whatever cause they may be referred, or however accounted for, are simply facts. The two classes of productions, by human art and by nature's forces, are alike in this great significant feature—in the fact of adaptation. In the case of structures by man, we *know* the adaptations to be the result of a cause working from the beginning to the predetermined end, and we *know* that cause to be an intelligent design. The similar *effect*, namely, adaptation, is by inductive analogy referred to a similar cause. Mind, intelligent will, is the only known cause of such effects, and we are thus necessitated to account for them, if we attempt to account for them at all, by such a reference. It is indeed objected that while this process is valid in reference to the products of man's industry, because we here actually perceive the working agent, it is not valid in the attempt to find a designer for nature, because the being of God, as the assumed agent, is unknown. But the demand for a suitable cause is direct and immediate from the observed fact of adaptation, and is not at all dependent on our previous knowledge of the agent or his manner of working. The analogical process moves back along the line of the causal law, and *finds* a predetermining agency in an intelligent purpose. The movement takes us *to* an agent. When once we have found the principle of final cause in our own psychical experience, and have become acquainted with the peculiar products of mental causation, we are furnished with the data for the analogical conclusion. The mind necessarily recognizes the work of mind wherever it stands in its presence. A thinking agent recognizes the products of thought. The finding of adaptation in mechanism, and belief in an intelligent cause for it, do not depend on a previous knowledge of the particular and competent agent.

The action of final cause, moreover, is a very large phenomenon on the earth. It is not simply an occasional or a feeble agency. In human industry design has determined, and still unceasingly determines, the appearance of the world and the course of events. It changes the face of the continents and islands of the sea, builds cities, binds nations together by railroads and telegraphs, and produces most of the wonderful effects which furnish the immediate conditions of human comfort and enjoyment. Most of the things in which life finds elevation and glory are unquestionably from the action of final cause in human activity. It must be noted distinctly that by using the established physical forces and laws, it brings about ten thousands of results which would never occur without it. Through science and invention it is making the world of to-day wear a different face from that of the old centuries. Through domestication of plants and animals, and enforced conditions of life, it regulates even the development of natural phenomena. The fact of design, furnishing analogy for the explanation of adaptations, is one of the most thoroughly known and impressive facts in the world. Not only is it known to be a real and actual cause of them, but it is the *only* known cause of them. To suppose them to be possibly due to something else, would be to abandon legitimate reasoning and resort to gratuitous conjecture. It would be to refuse a known and competent cause in favor of an unknown possibility; to reject that for which we have a reason in favor of that for which we have none.

There is another consideration which thoroughly justifies the principle of analogy here. This is that the human activities and industries which exhibit final causes in actual operation, themselves belong to the aggregate system of nature. The objection that discredits the validity of the reasoning has proceeded mainly on the idea, surreptitiously fetched in, that in finding final cause in the adaptations of nature, we unwarrantably take a fact and explanation from one realm and apply it to quite another and opposite realm. An impassable gulf is inserted between man and nature. We are told that we have no right, simply from knowing a cause of adaptations in intelligent human mechanics, to attribute the like cause to nature which shows no intelligence. But the objection turns to nothing, when the truth is remembered that man is not outside of nature or in antithesis to it. Whatever view may be taken of him, he is part of nature, the summit and crown of it, to be sure, but still embraced and held in it. He is born, and grows, and is dependent on the same chemical and physical laws as the animal world about him. He is subject to the common laws of organic life. Even his mental life is at present conditioned in the healthy action of a complex of natural forces. Thus, however clearly his possession of reason may suggest to faith a connection with a higher sphere, the roots of his being undoubtedly connect him with the great aggregate of nature. And it is to be specially noted that whatever view some thinkers may take of man in consideration of his power of free self-determination and spiritual destiny, those who deny final cause and the existence of God are emphatic in the complete identification of man with nature. To them he is simply a natural phenomenon, only and utterly a product and part of nature. Should others make a distinction between natural and human action, they allow none. Final cause in human art, therefore, furnishes not only an *analogon* for final cause in nature, but an *instance* of it. It presents a unique but actual example, of wide extent, in the midst of nature. When, therefore, we attribute it to nature, it is no gratuitous transfer of what belongs to one realm to another and distinct realm, but the simple extension of a principle which nature owns, and adopts in its highest range. Human industry is confessedly the action of final cause, and human industry belongs to nature. It is grotesquely absurd when men who see in our race nothing but an evolution of physical forces, but who effect adaptations by design every day, yet deny that nature exhibits final cause or predetermined products.

But without further vindicating here the validity of the conclusion reached by the application of analogy and induction in this argument, and thus anticipating what belongs to a later stage of this discussion, we simply call attention to the fact that the argument proceeds upon these principles, and that they are the recognized and accepted principles of science and practical life. If analogy and induction are valid for truth in other relations, it would be difficult to show why it should not be in this. In no other relation in all the wide range of human search after truth, are the facts underlying and impelling the inductive process and warranting its sufficiency so numerous and absolutely certain. If there is anything of which men are absolutely sure, it is the reality of this principle, as the explanation of known and intentionally produced adaptations. As the products of intelligent will-force, using efficient causes or natural laws for specific and useful ends, these adaptations mark the whole world of human industry and art. The peculiar products of final cause, the coordination that are due to design and mark it to intelligent observation, are the most familiar and unmistakable things of daily life. By an unquestionable experience design has been given us as the explanation of facts of adaptation, and the only explanation. We thus know this as a true, proper, competent cause of them, and we know of no other cause. And this proof proposes to show that *nature* abounds with adaptations, clear coordination of physical forces and processes to predetermined ends, which at once and directly reveal the working of an ordaining intelligence. They are recognized as the unmistakable work of a Thinker. While mind *is* known as the actual cause of adaptations to useful ends, in the uniform experience of the race, no other cause whatever is known. We have no knowledge of a contrary analogy, no example for a different induction. The evidence all points one way. It would be strange logic to refuse the conclusion to which all the evidence points for one wholly without evidence. Because analogy may fall short of a full demonstration, shall we therefore prefer a contrary conclusion not only utterly destitute of proof, but at war with all the real evidence in the case?

6. This proof considers the phenomena of the world as *effects,* *i.e.*, as "events," not as something self-existent and eternal, but as things which had a beginning, which once were not, but have

come to be. We are fully aware that it has been objected here that this is one of the chief points to be proved in order to justify the theistic conclusion. In former days, at least, the world itself was by some considered as self-existent and eternal. But while we freely consent that this point shall be held open to revision, if truth require, and that it shall have to be sustained by just evidence, we are fully warranted in at once conducting the argument on this idea, for the following reasons:

First, the entire evidence of the *cosmological argument* presents the world as an effect or a begun existence. The most careful and scrutinizing search can find nothing in the material universe either infinite or unconditioned. Limited and dependent forces and contingent forms alone are found in its phenomena, whether viewed in the aggregate or in its parts. The teleological argument starts with all the evidence gained in the cosmological conclusion.

Secondly, the special and particular phenomena considered in the teleological evidence are all *known to be caused* phenomena. Indeed, they are universally conceded to be "events" or "effects" in the fullest sense of the term. If there was ever a time when this could have been plausibly questioned or denied, science has now put that time forever in the past. It leaves no place for the old notion that the earth is eternal. Science finds none of its phenomena without a beginning, none that are not effects. It rigorously demands that, without exception, they all be considered as held under the law of causality. It opens the geologic records, and points to a time when the plants and animals that now are were not; when the races they belong to were not. It goes back and tells us, from evidences that allow no doubt, how and where the hills and mountains that seem most "everlasting" were made; how the rocks were built from the detritus of earlier rocks and by myriad animalcules working in the seas, and how the coal beds were formed of the forests. It is disposed even to go back further still—though probably only in a bold and brilliant hypothesis—and tell us how the earth, sun, moon, and planets were all formed out of nebular fire-mist. Seeing the overwhelming evidence that all earth-phenomena are not eternal, but caused or originated, science is thus, in all its working theories, now fully consenting at least to this point of theistic doctrine, that there was a time when the worlds were not. It joins in saying that they had a beginning and are effects. And these effects or "events" form the whole realm which the teleological argument investigates, and in which the evidence of final cause is traced. Even the notion of an "eternal series" fails to introduce any difficulty in the conditions of this proof. For. by very conception of an "eternal series," every event of the series becomes an effect. And if this effect exhibit final cause, the full basis for the teleological conclusion is there.

Thirdly, we may rightly start with this assumption, because in the evidence which it gives that the phenomena are really *products of thought*, this argument itself furnishes the invincible proof on this point. It proposes to show that they are *predetermined* products or existences, the reason of whose coordination and adaptations is not in the things themselves, and, therefore, *originated* phenomena, with an intelligent, preordaining mind behind them. The teleological evidence which makes it impossible to look on the world and its events as merely "the eternal stream of a planless coming and going," and compels us to regard its specific and wonderful adaptations as due to intelligent design, becomes itself the direct and final proof on this point. What is at the beginning taken as true, on the authority of observation and science, is in the end confirmed by the unique facts which the argument itself brings into convincing view.

7. Under the authority and guidance of these principles *two distinct points are to be proved. First, the reality of final causes, i.e., causes acting for ends, in nature*; and secondly, *that these are to be referred to an ordaining intelligence*. One gives us the great fact, the other the interpretation of it. Superficial thought often fails to keep these two things distinct. This is, indeed, not surprising, since they are really very closely allied. But they furnish basis for different classes of objections, or at least for objections in different senses. For example, Hume's objection, repeated by J. S. Mill and others, that we have no right to assume that nature acts in the production of her works as man does in the production of his, may mean either that there is no final cause at all in nature where there seems to be, but only consequences, or results, or

that though nature presents real final cause, we are not obliged to credit it, as we do in human industry, to intelligence or self-conscious will. In the one sense the objection doubts, or denies, the reality of nature's working for the sake of ends; in the other it implies that, for aught we know, there may be some *other* cause than *mind* for coordinated adaptations. It may be that in our common way of thinking specifically ordered adaptations and an intelligent designer stand as necessary correlates; but since there are those who assert that it is an unwarranted assumption when we make "mind," which is, indeed, *a* cause of adaptations, to be the *only possible* cause for them, it becomes necessary to keep in view this distinction between the fact of final cause and the interpretation of the fact. Usually, indeed, atheists deny both the fact and the interpretation, both *finality* and *intentionality*. For the sake of reaching an unassailable conclusion, both points must be sustained by adequate proof. They form the several premises of the evidence, as is shown whenever the teleological argument is reduced to syllogistic form, as, for instance:

> "Whatever exhibits marks of design had an intelligent author;
> The world exhibits marks of design;
> Therefore the world had an intelligent author."

We will, therefore, in the following sections present, first, some evidence that sustains the minor premise, or that nature exhibits causes acting for ends, and then examine the legitimacy of the interpretation which refers them to an intelligent author.

Natural Theology

SECTION II

THE REALITY OF FINAL CAUSES IN NATURE

The first and leading point in this whole argument is in the question: *Does nature exhibit causes acting for ends?* We adopt the term "finality" to designate the precise thing inquired after in this question. The point, let it be kept in mind, is not whether we can account for nature's pursuit of ends except by referring it to mind or intelligent purpose, but whether there *are* ends or objects really predetermined, sought and accomplished by nature—whether there is anywhere anything for the sake of which (the τὸ οὗ ἕνεκα of Aristotle) nature's processes work or its structures are produced. It may, indeed, be difficult to repress or keep back the idea of *intentionality*, or intelligent authorship, where we find finality or causes really regulated by ends; but in this section, and for the present, this is held in abeyance, and the inquiry is simply concerning finality. Whether or not this finality demands the recognition of mind as its cause is a question for further investigation.

The present inquiry, it must be further observed and remembered, is not at all a matter of speculation or interpretation, but simply and purely a question of fact. And the affirmation we make is that finality, or the action of causes for ends, *is a fact*, a fact prevailingly present in the constitution and processes of nature. For the sake of showing and illustrating this, we will gather a sufficient number of examples from the various departments in which nature offers itself to our inspection, in the following order: 1, in Organisms; 2, in Instinct; 3, in the General

Order of the Physical World; 4, in the Chemical Elements, and 5, in Mind.

ORGANISMS

1. Begin with the classic example of the *eye*. The question is: Does nature act for an end in the structure of this organ? Is it produced by chance or under final cause? Examine it. It is found to have all the parts and adaptations of a complete optical instrument, adjusted according to the laws of light for needed, comfortable and pleasurable vision. We have, first, a firm case, formed of several membranes, suited to hold all the parts, upon which are fastened the cords and pulleys of its skilful mounting and motion. The outer of these membranes, called the *sclerotic*, is opaque on the back and sides of the eye, but in front suddenly becomes transparent as crystal, and so forms the *cornea*—or, rather, it terminates in a bevelled edge which receives the cornea as a watch-glass is received by the grooves in its case. Within this is a second coating, which becomes thoroughly opaque in the front, forming the *iris*, through which no ray of light can pass except by the opening in the center, known as the *pupil*. This iris is a self-adjusting network, which no skill of man can equal, enlarging or diminishing the pupil according to the intensity of the light, and always in a perfect circle. Within the case are the different humors, the aqueous, the crystalline, and the vitreous, forming together a compound lens, of finest refracting power. Piercing the double coating on the rear, a fine thread comes forth from the brain, and spreads itself out on the deep interior of the eye as a delicate coating, or screen, known as the *retina*, or optic nerve expansion, upon which the light, reflected from external objects and refracted through the lenses, falls, producing there an image of those objects, as in a *camera obscura*. The formation of this image is essential to sight, and the result is actually accomplished through this lengthened, complex and elaborate combination of parts, in which is brought together a great variety of materials, of the exact qualities and quantity needed, and in position clearly adapted to this single end. But more than this

must be considered. This instrument, so exactly optical on mechanical principles, is put into a place clearly adapted for it. A cavity is provided in the bone, with grooves and perforations for the necessary machinery of motion. The eye is packed in soft elastic cushions, and fastened by strings and pulleys, to give it ease, variety, and rapidity of motion. A delicate fringe of lashes, that never needs clipping, helps to guard it, while not obstructing the light. Above this a projecting brow is formed, furnishing additional defense. And what is most suggestive of prearranged plan—near the eye is a laboratory, called a gland, put up and kept running, to secrete a suitable fluid to keep the whole organ moist and comfortable, with a pipe laid to conduct the fluid to its place.

Now it is a simple matter of fact, and not in any just sense a speculative opinion, that the eye thus described is a constructed instrument, whose parts are adapted to a fixed, definite, and consistently pursued end. It is a complex organ, in which nature is plainly and actually accomplishing a precise and determined object. We are not, in this statement, interpreting any merely subjective notion of our own into the eye, but simply stating what it *is* as a structured part of nature. In it organization of various materials and parts into an instrument of vision, is simply a fact. It is a complex of adaptations to an actual end—an end to which all the efficient causation producing the eye is unquestionably correlated. In other words, it is really an "organ." If it is not this it is no eye at all, the very concept of the eye having dropped away. We press the emphasis on this point, that adaptation of the structure to vision is purely a matter of fact, as truly so as is the existence of the parts which compose it. Whatever explanation may be given of it, nature is here actually pursuing an end for the service of the entire animal and human worlds.

Our impression of this truth is yet further deepened when we consider more specifically such things as these: (1) That vision is a necessity for the whole purpose and work of man on earth, something so important that the failure of it would bar off the race from all the high life for which it finds its lofty faculties to be suited. (2) That this need, being developed only as a result of the completed organization of man's faculties and of his position, could be efficient for the origination of the eye only as a final cause. (3) That in the eye *independent* things the most remote from each other, as light from the sun and the refractive power of certain humors, are made to *concur* in a definite and exact result suited to the perceiving mind. (4) That not only is every part of the structure complete in itself, but it is accurately and fixedly adapted not only to every other, but to the final result, the absence of any one part being destructive of the use of the whole. (5) That there is nothing in the nature of the elements themselves found to compose the matter of the eye, considered as chemical constituents, to necessitate or account for their running into this particular structure just in the place occupied by this organ. And (6) that this instrument in every instance of the millions and millions of human beings and animals, is prepared and made ready for use in advance and by anticipation, an instrument constructed and formed in the dark for the time of light. When all these points are considered in connection with the extremely artificial forms and features of the organ, already mentioned, such as the opaque sclerotic changed to transparency in front, the iris with its pupil for admission of the light, the genuine lenses, the outspread optic nerve, the adjusted pulleys and cords for motion, and the factory and pipes for the moistening fluid, all put and kept together for the mind's use, it is impossible rationally to doubt that we have here a case where nature's work is pursuing and actually accomplishing a distinct and definite end. We have a very fact of finality—the function of vision provided for by a special structure or instrument arranged to afford it. If this is not to be accepted as a very fact of nature, we know not on what basis science is justified in claiming any of its data as facts.

2. The *ear*, as the organ of hearing, deserves to be mentioned next after the eye. It is as well adapted to its purpose as is the organ of sight. Though not quite so complex and wonderful as the eye, it consists as truly of distinct structures and adjusted parts, all brought into peculiar and specific relations, and accurately arranged for giving to the soul communication with the outer world. The external part is an admirable formation for collecting the vibrations of the air and conducting them inward. If this is not its object, no explanation why it exists can be given.

The continuous channel, the bony rim with tympanum stretched over it, the several additional bones leading further inward, arranged like a well contrived telephonic line, the eustachian tube supplying air for the inner cavities, all together exhibit nature as working out a specific and well defined purpose. The whole organ is as complete an adaptation of a complex of peculiarly formed parts to the laws of sound or the vibratory action of the air, and turning it to the service of the mind, as is the eye to the laws of light. Can anyone account for the formation of the ear, an organ so differentiated and fixed into permanency of specific structure, except as called for under a law of ends in nature's system? Does it not present a real fact of structural adaptation to a necessary use?

3. In the other senses, *taste, smell,* and *touch*, we find similar provision for necessities in the animal economy. Each one presents a specific organization adjusted to a particular function serviceable to the animal life. In the case of taste and smell there is a localization of unique structure in which special provision occurs, furnishing a means of information to the mind concerning the outer world. There is no reason whatever to think that it is an essential property of matter to organize itself into papillae for taste or smell, since each occurs only on a particular spot in the animal surface. Nor are these organs, or the sense-perceptions through them, so essential to animal life that they may be looked upon as "necessary conditions of existence." The sense of *touch*, indeed, is spread over almost the entire surface; but on that surface it nevertheless appears as a particular nerve structure, a specific provision, with the finest actual adaptation to the wants and welfare of the whole man. It forms a marvelous adjustment to all the great purposes or activities to which we find our aggregate nature calling us in life. If we leave the idea of ends out of view, there is no conceivable reason why matter should evolve, just where it would be useful, a structure so unique and marvelously suited to serve every part of the complex bodily organism.

4. The *bony framework* of man and of all animals presents a wonderfully impressive instance of nature's acting for ends. This is true in every aspect in which it may be viewed. Looked at simply as a particular *substance,* concreted in the process of

growth, it is remarkably fitted for building the skeleton or frame for the rest of the body. Considered as so framed together, the purposive features become strikingly apparent. Each bone has a special structure, as to length, thickness, figure, curve, or notch, after the manner of a specifically prepared piece. Each one bears this feature as plainly as do the plates and bars and bolts and screws which the machinist forms to make an engine or a printing press. Most artificially formed joints are found connecting these various pieces—about two hundred and eighteen in the human frame—providing for the kind and degree of motion required everywhere by the principles of both utility and beauty. In these joints, strong ligaments, skilfully inserted, tie the bones securely together. A good example of this is seen in the firm yet flexible cord in the hip joint, inserted at one end in the head of the ball and at the other in the cup of the socket, and holding them securely against liability of dislocation. A more remarkable illustration is found in the knee joint, where two ligaments are used and additional security is gained by their being made to cross each other. This ligamental binding is no new method, or one developed only in the human frame. Fossil evidence from the old geological formations exhibits instances, even in marine life, of the ball-and-socket joint of exquisite workmanship, with the ligament to unite the parts. As a special method of attaining this end, it seems to have originated as soon as the general plan of animal organization called for it, and it has continued through untold ages as the permanent form of contrivance for security in the jointing. Its origin cannot possibly be attributed to the mechanical action of the parts, as that action manifestly tends to destroy rather than create such ligaments. It can be taken as a "survival of the fittest" only when credited to the action of a creative and controlling Will.

No artificer could plan and put together on mathematical principles a more distinctly adapted framework than this bony structure as a whole. In whatever modifications it is found in the various animal races, an orderly method holds throughout, a method which not only provides a solid firm support for the various parts of the body, but protecting covering for the most important organs, such as the brain, the heart, the lungs, and the digestive apparatus, and furnishes attachment for hundreds of cords that are to give it motion, while it presents perforations here and there for the passage of nerves, veins, and arteries. The question is: Does this framework present a real adaptation of part to part and of the whole to a specific end in the animal economy? Is it only a result of coincidence in the blind movement of efficient forces not at all designed to produce this result, or are the parts and the whole what they are for the sake of the organization? It seems to me that a man must throw away all known and accepted principles of sound judgment or rational perception, to deny the fact of finality here.

5. The *muscles* exhibit adaptation unmistakably. This is apparent whether considered as to their intrinsic structure or their location and order of attachment. Singly and in itself each muscle bears evident marks of being made for an end. It is composed of fasciculi, or bundles of fibers of variable size. These are enclosed in a cellular membranous investment or sheath. Each of the constituent fibers consists of a number of filaments. Toward the extremity of the muscle the muscular fiber ceases and the cellular structure becomes aggregated, and so modified as to constitute *tendons*, by which it is tied to the bone. The peculiar characteristic of muscular fiber is *contractility*, or the power of shortening length on command of the will or from the application of external stimuli. The contraction is toward the middle of the muscle. When the stimulus is withdrawn the muscle is again relaxed. By this particular property it is at once suited to the service of producing motion. The fact of adaptation in a saw for cutting wood is not plainer or more real than that of a muscle for moving the bones and parts of the body.

Taken together, and considered especially as to their location and points of origin and insertion, their subservience to a plan and use is, if possible, still more evident. The disposition and point of attachment are always such that the contraction gives the direction and degree of motion needful for the convenient action and use of every part and of the entire body. For instance, the different muscles which move the arm are so tied to the three chief bones of its skeleton, and continued by the tendons extending into the hand, that by the pull of their simple contraction they furnish all the motions required for the activities, industries, and arts of life.

And very remarkable it certainly is that the muscle is always found exactly fitted to the particular kind and degree of motion to which the special joint is adapted. Where the bones are united by a hinge joint, the muscles are arranged only for the motion for which that form of joint provides. Where there is a ball-and-socket joint, the muscles are inserted so as to give the rotary motion. There are more than five hundred muscles in the human body; and everywhere, in their size, length, and places of attachment, the principle of specific adjustment, not only to the most varied particulars of the bony frame, but to the necessities of every other part of the bodily organization, is most conspicuously observable. In many places, as, for example, to secure the needed motion of the eye, or the delicate cunning of the fingers, anatomy exhibits the result as accomplished by what strikes the mind as a thoroughly studied, complicated, artistic contrivance.

6. The *digestive system*, though very complex, and in some respects remote from inspection, when thoroughly studied and understood is seen to be an impressive instance in which nature is made to act for a definite end, beginning a needed process and carrying it through a long series of provisions to its completion in the nourishment of the whole body. Let us briefly follow it out. The digestive organs are the mouth, the teeth, the salivary glands, the pharynx, œsophagus, stomach, intestines, lacteals, thoracic duct, liver, and the pancreas.

The mouth, with the teeth and salivary glands, is adapted to the mastication and softening of foods. It forms a needful mill, put up at the commencement of the process. Through the pharynx and œsophagus a channel is provided for passing the prepared food into the stomach. Special muscles are furnished to perform the act of swallowing, and the food and drink are prevented from entering into the trachea or windpipe by a valve-like arrangement called the epiglottis. The stomach into which the food is delivered—and no carrying company could show a better organization for delivery—is furnished with a peculiar fluid called the gastric juice, a powerful solvent of inimitable kind, secreted by the gastric gland. Harmless to the coats of the stomach, this gastric fluid attacks and dissolves all the various substances suitable for food. Though manufactured regularly, through all the years of life, by the gastric gland, no human chemistry has been able to compound or produce it. Its action reduces the foods to a pulpy homogeneous mass, of creamy consistence, called *chyme*. From the stomach the *pylorus* forms an orifice conducting the chyme into the *duodenum*, where, from the liver and pancreas, bile and pancreatic fluid are added, changing the chyme into *chyle* and residuum. In the duodenum and other parts of the small intestine a most remarkable arrangement is found, known as the *lacteals*. These are very minute vessels or openings in the mucous surface of the intestine, passing thence between the membranes of the *mesentery* to small glands, which they enter. There are several ranges of these glands. The first range collects many of the small vessels, and transmits a few larger ones to a second range. After passing through several successive ranges of these glands the lacteals, diminished in number but increased in size, proceed to the thoracic duct into which they open. As the chyle is moved over the mucous surface of the small intestine and comes in contact with these lacteal vessels, it is imbibed or taken up by them as through a filter, and passed on thence into the thoracic duct. This duct commencing in the abdomen, forms a continuous channel, passing upward through the diaphragm and ascending to the lower part of the neck, where it makes a sudden turn downward and forward, terminating by opening into a large vein which enters the heart. Carried up this channel, the chyle is poured into and mixed with the old blood at this point. Valves opening in the direction of the proper movement, but closing in the opposite, are parts of the elaborate arrangement for the long process.

Looking at all this, and remembering the need to be provided for, namely, the preparation and change of the proper substances for the nourishment and growth of the body, the adaptation of the means to the end becomes clear and certain. We see a complex and extended system, composed of separate and independent organs, brought, by special structure and place, into concurrent action, and made to cooperate in a result to which the first step looks as plainly as the last. A needful thing was before nature, and nature has been made to seek and accomplish the needful thing.

7. The *circulatory organs* are for the distribution of the blood to every part of the body. They are the heart, arteries, veins, and capillaries. These are so connected as to form a continued series, with functions constituting a complete circle. The heart stands at the beginning, and is clearly a piece of nature's mechanism for a purpose. It is a double organ, or has two sides called the right and left. Each side is also divided into two parts. It is composed of peculiar fiber, with strong contractile power, the two sides and the two cavities of each side working in corresponding action under the impulse of a special nerve organization. One side of the heart is so arranged as to receive the mixture of old blood and chyle from the large vein which enters there, and to pass it through the lungs; the other to take it and force it again into the body through the arteries, for the nourishment and upbuilding of the system. By its automatic action, the provision for which is so strange a fact of its muscular and nervous structure, the heart is a pump of immense force, with pipes and valves finely constructed and connected. It forms a conspicuous instance of adaptation—an organ put together, in nature's growth, on mechanical principles, to effect a specific and unquestionable end in the animal economy.

The completion of the circulatory process is provided for in the arteries, capillaries, and veins. The arteries, for carrying the blood from the heart, under the strong pressure with which it is forced into them, are made of strong material and laid deep as a necessary precaution for safety, while the veins in which there is little pressure are weaker and less guarded. The capillaries constitute a microscopic network, and are so distributed to every part of the body as to make it impossible to insert a needle point beneath the skin without wounding some of them. They unite at the one end with the terminal extremities of the arteries, and at the other with the commencement of the veins, establishing thus a communication between the arteries and veins, or the outward and returning flow of the blood. The valves, set at various points in the veins as well as in the heart, to prevent a reflow of the blood, are remarkable exhibitions of nature's mechanics, and so clearly exist in a relation of means to a specific end that they disclosed to Harvey the great law of the circulation of the blood. The whole circulatory apparatus, consisting thus of the heart, arteries, and veins, constitutes a structure as clearly planned for carrying the blood from the heart, distributing it to every part of the body, and returning it again for oxygenation, mixed with the fresh chyle, as is the system of pipes planned, by which water is not only conducted into an engine and turned into power there, but conducted off, and, after condensation, returned again to the point of origin to repeat the round of service.

8. The *lungs* bear equal testimony that nature correlates her organizations to particular ends. The animal economy being in other respects as it is, the aeration of the blood is a needful function. The organ for effecting this is formed and placed in immediate connection with the heart. "The lungs, as is well known, consist of two large organs, on either side of the chest, called the left and the right lungs. The right lung is divided into three smaller lungs, called lobes; the left into but one or two. On examining any of these lobes it will be found to be made up of an immense number of small membranous bags, all closely packed together. These bags, called cells, connect by means of the bronchial tubes and windpipe with the air through the nose and mouth. They vary in size, but on an average are about of an inch in diameter, and the total number of the cells in the lungs has been estimated at six hundred millions. Their walls are exceedingly thin, and the cells may therefore be easily compressed. The whole mass of the lungs is also exceedingly elastic, and by the action of a system of muscles their volume is alternately increased and diminished in the process of respiration. The amount of air which is thus drawn into the cells and again expelled at each inspiration differs in different individuals. The average quantity in the ordinary tranquil respiration of an adult is about a pint; but in a full respiration it may be as much as two and a half pints, and by an effort the lungs may be made to inhale from five to seven pints. As the average in health is about eighteen inspirations a minute, which corresponds to about eighteen pints of air inhaled and exhaled, it follows that three

thousand gallons of air pass through the lungs of an adult man every day." When the blood, freshly charged with the inflowing chyle, is received from the large vein into the heart, it is pumped thence through the pulmonary artery into the lungs. This artery divides and branches, all through the lungs, into very small capillary tubes which ramify on the surface of the air-cells. In these capillaries, formed of the thinnest conceivable membranes, the blood is brought into such close relation to the air as to absorb the oxygen needed to prepare it for its great function of nourishment. Thus prepared, it is returned by a series of veins to the left side of the heart, by which it is again forced through the general circulation of the body. The peculiar organization and connections of the lungs, especially their connection with the heart as a distinct but cooperating organ, form a clear and unquestionable adjustment of means to an end.

9. The process of *nutrition*, accomplished through the digestive, the respiratory, and the circulatory organs, deserves to be briefly recalled. This is the change of the elements in the blood into the various substances which compose the body. Under the wonderful chemistry of animal life and by the action of the nutrient arteries, that is, the finest capillaries, these elements are transformed at every point into precisely what is there needed for repair of waste and for growth. The matter is not transformed and spread miscellaneously and indiscriminately anywhere and everywhere or at random, but deposited in exactest quality and quantity at the spot required by each part and by the balance and beauty of the parts and of the whole. Out of the same blood is formed at one place bone, at another muscular fibre, at another fat, at another nerve, at another nail, at another hair, in the precise measure and modification that accord with the plan of each organ and of the entire body. Where lime is wanted, lime is carried and deposited. Where silica is needed, silica is carried and left. Where iron, carbon, chlorine, or any element whatever is proper, there it is put. So the constant waste is repaired or the growth is carried on in the nicest proportion for utility and for beauty. Does not all this exhibit nature's processes looking to specific ends and accomplishing them? Account for it as we may, the process or work of forming and building up the body goes on,

the differentiation of the parts occurring from the common blood, with all the nice discrimination of means for ends and with all the steady adherence to the ideals of a fixed plan that the most intelligent and forecasting scientist can display in the best productions of the laboratory.

10. A very illustrative organization is found in the *ankle*. This is the arrangement binding down the tendons there by a ligament passing over them. The foot is placed at a considerable angle with the leg. As a consequence of this, the flexible tendons passing from the leg to the toes, if unsecured, when the muscle contracts, would start away from the ankle. But they are prevented by a clearly precautionary arrangement. A strong ligament is stretched across the instep, tying them securely down. Cut the ligament and the tendons will start up. It is a plain instance of a bandage to effect the specific end of keeping the cords in place. And it is to be observed that here, as in many other structures, there can be no conceivable tendency in the part itself toward self-creation or continuance in existence. The function it fulfils would tend rather to the destruction and disappearance of the part.

11. The organs for the perpetuation of the various animal species exhibit one of the most striking and incontrovertible cases of which we know, in which nature's organization is directed to a predetermined end. These organs, in addition to the directness with which their design is assured, have this remarkable peculiarity that the corresponding parts of them belong to different individuals. The adaptation includes an adjustment of structural provision in separate beings. This provision made for the perpetuation of the human and the animal races allows no rational explanation without the admission of final cause. Science utterly fails to eliminate design from the structure and function of these organs, or even to describe and explain their parts except in terms that express design, purpose, or ends.

2. It is unnecessary to multiply examples of finality, of this class. They may be seen everywhere. The few instances given represent the truth for the whole of organic nature. We add only one more illustration, in the structure of birds. And we simply quote here from Prof. Chadbourne: "The whole bird tribe is a

marvel of special adaptations. The whole external structure which characterizes birds is a special adaptation to the external world; and when we consider the means by which this perfect relationship is secured, we are delighted by the skill manifested in the whole plan, and the perfection with which that plan is carried out. Flight is secured by the most skilful mechanism of feathers, and the accumulation of muscle around the shoulder of the bird. What can be more perfect in its mechanism than each feather of the wing—its hollow elastic shaft securing lightness and strength? Then we have the skilful joining of all the lines of the web, and the combination of barbs and hooks that has ever challenged the admiration of men. The position of all the feathers is such that by expanding the wing they cover the greatest extent possible, with no openings between them. The muscles are not only of great strength, but they are so arranged that the wing strikes the air at the required angle to enable the bird to rise and completely control its motions. And then observe the compactness with which the instrument is folded away when not in use. The great expenditure of muscular force is provided for by the great lung capacity, the whole viscera even being bathed with air. The bird by instinct trims its feathers, when the web has been broken; and because the feathers are too long, and not of a structure like hair, to receive from the body the oil which they need to preserve their gloss, nature has provided a never failing bottle of oil on the back of the bird which instinct has taught it how to use."

13. The human or animal organization *must be considered as a whole*, or as a complex of various organs and parts. All these separate parts, each a complete organism in itself, are combined in action and function into a full unity and individuality. The plan that is seen in each part thus becomes more conspicuously unquestionable. The body, viewed as a whole, exhibits such a marvel of elaborate, skilful, and accurate contrivance, adapted to the service and enjoyment of life, as to call forth the admiration of thoughtful men in all ages. "The human body," said Galen, "is a perpetual hymn to the praise of its Maker." The point to be here specially noted is that finality, or parts acting for ends, is involved in the very concept of an organized being. Dr. Porter says, with evident truth: "An organic being, or an organism, can only be

defined as a being of which each organ acts for the integrity and well-being of every other organ, and all act together for the life of the whole. More abstractly and in the terms of the relation in question [the relation of final cause], an organism is a being in which each part and the whole are respectively means and end for one another. We find it, in fact, to be true that in every living being, whether plant or animal, the elements or organs act together so as to promote the action of each other and of the whole. If the appropriate function of each organ is performed, the function of every other is also fulfilled, and when all together are exerted they are the conditions of the growth and development of the plant or animal. In the animal the action of the lungs is necessary to that of the heart, and the action of the heart to that of the lungs, the action of both to the action of the stomach, and the action of the stomach to both of these, and the mutual action of these and the remaining organs to the health and life of the body." And we must add that neither the separate parts with their functions, nor the united organism with its action can be rationally accounted for by efficient causation alone, nor even defined by its terms. The elements of which the organism is composed have their well ascertained mechanical and chemical properties, and when they are combined in non-living or inorganic substances, they exhibit only the action of these properties and their laws. But in the production of organisms and their correlation to the special interests of living beings, the causal action of these elements is clearly transcended. Neither the tissues nor the "cells" to which physiology seeks to trace organic structures, nor the chemical powers and laws of the elements in themselves, serve at all to explain these results, except as presided over and directed by a predetermining and correlating thought. The relation of means to end is therefore not only an unquestionable fact in organisms, but a fact insoluble by the simple causal force of the known properties of the elements.

INSTINCT

To understand the bearing of *instinct* on the question of finality in nature, we must recall what instinct is, and its relation to mere organization and function on the one hand, and to intelligence on the other.

Instinct may properly be defined to be an effective blind tendency in animals toward specific kinds of action for self-preservation and the continuance of the species, regulative of the appetites and of various functional capacities. Under it animals act without experience or training. They pursue a course of wisdom and intelligence without themselves exercising any calculating judgment, or understanding the ends to be accomplished by their action. It has no free choice. Operating by some innate or constitutional impulse, it works, in like conditions, in the same manner in all the individuals of each species. Its action is uniform in the same circumstances. If any deviation appears to occur, the change or modification is provided for in the aggregate law of instinct. It is only diverted by circumstances, the deviation being itself as truly under law as is deviation of organism from ordinary form in the same species. "In proportion as instinct predominates, we may predict with certainty the action of the individual, when we know the life-history of the species; its whole aim being to work out a design which is formed *for* it, not *by* it, and the tendency to which is embodied, as it were, in its organization." "An animal is already all that it is through its instinct; a reason foreign to it, the reason of another, has already made every provision for it, while man uses his own reason." Schopenhauer says: "The aim toward which animals work so directly in the acts of instinct, as if it were a known motive, remains entirely unknown to them." Darwin states the generally accepted idea of instinct: "An action, which we ourselves should require experience to enable us to perform, when performed by an animal, more especially by a very young one, without any experience, and when performed by many individuals in the same way, without their knowing for what purpose it is performed, is usually said to be *instinctive*."

The relation of instinct to mere *structure and organic function* is readily and clearly distinguishable. Organisms have functions which they fulfil by mere force of the material or vital organization. This order of action is found even in the vegetable kingdom. It is one of the features which distinguish the vegetable realm from the inorganic. As soon as nature rises into the organic realm, in plant life, we find specialized structures with distinct functions. Not only do the elements, under the laws of growth, move as if marshalled under an ordaining and directing intelligence into the formation of organs and organisms, but these organs are found fulfilling certain needful functions for the perfection of the plant or the perpetuation of the species. The processes which take place in the springing corn or the growing oak act for the completion of the plant or tree and the preparation of seed for future growths. This principle of organ and function, thus begun in the vegetable kingdom, is continued in the higher range of animal life. It is seen and illustrated in the action of the heart, the lungs, the secretory processes of the glands, and in all reflex nerve motion. Instinct is something superadded to this, supplementing it in further provision for the animal's own needs and welfare and the continuance of the race. There are some animals so low in the scale of being that they appear to possess no instinct at all, or very little, and to be but slightly organic or vitalized masses. Simple function appears to be the whole of their life-activity—function not much above that in the organism of a wheat stalk or an apple tree. This may be illustrated in the case of a clam or an oyster. Apparently, at least, it has no more conscious relation to its young than the tree has to its seed. "The production of its young is simply the result of organic change, the law of its growth, like the budding and blossoming of the tree."[2] The only indication of instinct about it appears in the moving or closing of its cell for self-preservation. Even this seems merely structural and automatic. But instinct is something different and higher than such directly functional action. It appears where in addition to this, and turning the possibilities which organs provide for into appropriate effect, specific impulse and guidance are supplied to animals both for the care of themselves and the needs of their offspring. It utilizes and directs the aggregate of organic functions to ulterior and higher ends. "Instinct supplements structure and functions, putting them to the best use, making a higher type of life possible than could be manifested by structure and function alone. The bee has a structure fitting it for gathering honey, and the rings of the body have the function of secreting wax. Instinct is needed to impel the bee to gather the honey and form the scales of wax into the honeycomb." Besides the organs and their functions, therefore, there is an added impulse, so strong that it becomes like a secret wheel in a system of machinery, which is so important that without it the entire machinery would fail.

The relation of instinct to animal *intelligence*, though in many respects difficult to be determined, is in the main easily recognized. Many animals seem to possess what may be termed intelligence. It is by this that they enter into conscious relations with man, understand his wishes, and cooperate with his aims. Some of them seem, at least in a measure, to comprehend what they do in these relations, and voluntarily concur in human plans and work. We do not call this part of animal capacity instinct. We call it "animal intelligence," whatever that may be. But the term "instinct" properly stands, not for this higher range of action often strikingly illustrated in special feats of sagacity, in which the domestic animals understand and serve men, but the inferior grade of blind movement supplementing functional activities, in which they act on fixed methods for self-preservation and the perpetuation of the race. "The character which, above all, distinguishes instinctive actions," says Milne-Edwards, "from those which may be called intelligent or rational, is that they are not the result of imitation and experience; that they are always executed in the same manner, and, to all appearance, without being preceded by the foresight either of their result or of their utility. Reason supposes a judgment and a choice; instinct, on the contrary, is a blind impulse which naturally impels the animal to act in a determinate manner; its effects may sometimes be modified by experience, but they never depend on it." Whatever explanation may be given of this force, whether it shall be found due to special sensations produced by environment or to reflex action analogous to that which impels organic motion itself, or to some other cause, it is a clearly supplemental provision carrying the complex of organic functions to their full appropriate results, and securing, through a non-intelligent and enforced activity, an intelligent and steady coordination of wise means to special, predetermined, and far-reaching ends. Blind powers have been organized to act as if they had pierced the future with a clear foresight of what would be needed, and with the most discriminating choice of the fitting way to accomplish it. The very powers and laws of nature, even such as recent science alone has been able to discover, have been taken into account in the adaptive processes through which instinct pursues its blind way to its unknown but appointed result.

A glance at the action of instinct in a few of its leading forms will be sufficient to explain and illustrate its bearing as a fact of clear finality in nature.

1. Some forms of it regulate the *choice of foods*. This is one of the lowest and simplest acts of instinct, joining closely on what is simply organic and arising out of it. Appetite, being properly only functional, craves, and instinct directs the action of this craving, so as to avoid what would be injurious and select what is nourishing. From the immense diversity of materials it picks out with steady accuracy those which have the right constituents, and which the digestive system has been prepared to use, each species of animals having its own foods, and its young selecting them at once. Without hint from the chemist's analysis of secret poisons, or instruction of any kind, instinct recognizes them and rejects them. In the lowest animal orders, as the *entozoa*, the food seems to be simply absorbed. But in the higher grades, it is selected under some exercise of the senses and perceptions. If it be said that this selection is simply from the sense of smell, each species being guided by what is pleasant to it, it is yet to be accounted for that the smell has been so precisely correlated to the animal's interests and safety, since "there is no necessary relation between the pleasure of an external sense and the needs of the internal organization."

The feeding instinct often involves *correspondent* action in several individuals. It is largely so among birds. The young bird, just hatched, raises its head and opens its bill. Its hunger impels to motion, and its instinct secures the right motion. But this would be in vain, if alone. The instinct of the mother bird, however, responds and brings the proper food. Without this correlation of instincts the young would perish.

When the eggs of the bee deposited in the cells are about to hatch, the worker-bees eagerly seek for that particular species of nourishment on which the larvæ are to feed. This consists of pollen with a proportion of honey and water, which is partly digested in the stomach of the bees, and made to vary in its quality according to the age of the young. As soon as the eggs are hatched, the bees feed the larvæ with great assiduity with this prepared chyle. When, from any cause, there has been a failure in the production of young queens, and it becomes necessary to raise a queen, the worker-bees, having placed eggs, or larvae not yet three days old, in enlarged cells, called "royal cells," supply these cells with a peculiar kind of food which appears to be more stimulating than that of ordinary bees. This is furnished to the royal larvæ in greater quantities than can be consumed, so that a portion always remains behind in the cell after transformation. By this kind of food, in the enlarged cells, the larvæ are developed into queen bees. Dr. Carpenter well says: "This last action is one which it is scarcely possible that either theory or experience could lead the bees to perform; for not the most ingenious reasoning could have anticipated the fact that by supplying a worker-larva with food of a different quality, and enlarging the cell around it, a change so remarkable should be produced in its structure, capacities, and instincts; and the circumstances of the case seem no less to forbid the notion that the bees owe a knowledge of the process to experimental researches carried on either by themselves or by their ancestors, for the purpose of securing an artificial supply of queens when the natural supply fails. That recourse is uniformly had to it whenever the case requires, has been repeatedly shown by experiment, the removal of the parent queen and of the royal larvæ from the hive being always followed by the manufacture, so to speak, of worker-larvæ into new queens. The *irrationality* of the impulse which prompts the bees to this action is evidenced by its occasional performance under circumstances which, if they could reason, would have shown them that it *must* be ineffective. A case has been recorded in which a queen, having only laid *drone* or male eggs, was stung to death by the workers, who cast her body out of the hive; but being thus left without a queen, and no royal larvæ being in process of development to replace her, the workers actually tried to obtain a queen by treating *drone* larvæ in the usual manner—of course without effect."

2. Some instincts are organized to the *preparation and storage of food*. This is rendered needful by the change of seasons. The action is illustrated in the well-known habits of bees, building suitable vessels and collecting and storing away honey by industrious anticipative labor. It is seen in the case of squirrels which gather nuts of various kinds, and make use of hollow trees or other available places as magazines. They sometimes make deposits at different places, which they are usually able afterward to find even in spite of the fall of snows. Various animals gather the ripe fruits of the earth and lay them up for food. A species of harvesting is often practiced. The Alpine hare of Mongolia is said to lay in a store of hay for winter use, collecting it at the end of summer, and stacking it, after being dried, at the entrance of its home. This serves for its couch underground, and for food till the return of spring. There are certain leaf-cutting ants which dry the collected leaves before taking them into their houses. Some ants harvest various seeds and store them away. "The Siberian rodent, *lagomys pica*, gathers autumn grass, cutting, drying, and putting it away like farmers gathering hay." Thus these, and many other species of animals, incapable of consciously foreseeing the need, yet provide for it in a course of action wisely, accurately, and uniformly adjusted to the ends.

3. Some instincts are adjusted to *building*, for the sake of both the individual and the species. "The most remarkable examples of instinctive action that the entire animal kingdom can furnish are presented in the operations of bees, wasps, ants, and other social insects which construct habitations for themselves upon a plan which the most enlightened human intelligence, working according to most refined geometrical principles, could not surpass; but which yet do so without education communicated by their parents or progressive attempts of their own, and with no trace of hesitation, confusion, or interruption, the several

individuals of a community all laboring effectively to one common end, because their instinctive or consensual impulses are the same."

The building operations of bees have been to all ages a wonder of blind impulse doing the work of knowledge and wisdom. Admiration never ceases at the regularity and accuracy with which their cells have been constructed to afford from the materials the greatest space for each cell, and admit of their being joined together on the same plane without leaving interstices. The mathematical determination of the order for the construction fulfilling the necessary conditions, though difficult, has often been made. Mr. Hunter, one of the highest authorities on the subject, tells us: "Reaumer proposed to König, pupil of the celebrated Bernouilli, and an expert analyst, the solution of the problem: To find the construction of a hexagonal prism terminated by a pyramid composed of three equal and similar rhombs (and the whole of given capacity), such that the solid may be made with the least quantity of materials—which involved the determination of the angles of the rhombs that should cut the hexagonal prism so as to form with it the figure of the least possible surface. Maraldi had previously measured the angles of the rhombus, and found them to be 109° 28′ and 70° 32′, respectively. But König was not aware of this until after he had solved the problem, and assigned 109° 26′ and 70° 34′ as the angles. The *Memoirs of the Academy of Science* for 1712, containing Maraldi's paper, was then sent to him, and König was equally surprised and pleased to find how nearly the actual measurement agreed with the result of his own investigation. The measurement of Maraldi is correct, and the bees have, with rigorous accuracy, solved the problem, for the error turns out to be in König's solution. The construction of cells, then, is demonstrated to be such that no other that could be conceived would take so little material and labor to afford the same room. Confirmatory solutions have been worked out by other mathematicians. But a more essential advantage than even the economy of wax results from this structure, namely, that the whole fabric has much greater strength than if it were composed of planes at right angles to one another; and when we consider the weight they have to support when stored with honey, pollen, and the young brood, besides that of the bees themselves, it is evident that strength is a material requisite in the work. It has often been a subject of wonder how such diminutive insects could have adopted and adhered to so regular a plan of architecture, and what principles can actuate so great a multitude to cooperate, by the most effectual and systematic mode, in its completion. Buffon attempted to explain the hexagonal form by the uniform pressure of a great number of bees, all working at the same time, equally exerted in all directions in a limited space. But his supposition is confuted by its being directly at variance with the actual process employed by the insects. It might be supposed that bees had been provided by nature with instruments for building, of a form somewhat analogous to the angles of the cells; but in no part, either of the teeth, antenna, or feet, can any such correspondence be traced. Their shape in no respect answers to that of the rhombs which are constructed by their means, any more than the chisel of the sculptor resembles the statue which it has carved. The shape of the head is, indeed, triangular, but its three angles are acute, and are different from that of the planes of the cells. The form of the plates of wax, as they are molded in the pouches in which this substance is secreted, is an irregular pentagon, in no respects affording a model for any of the parts which compose the honeycomb."

Everyone is familiar with the nest-building of birds. Each species builds in its own way, and the skilled ornithologist knows the bird by the nest. The bird that never saw a nest will construct one as all its tribe has done before it, selecting the same materials, if accessible, and putting them together in the same way. That it acts without deliberation and choice is evident from the fact that it acts with a uniformity which presents no more deviation than the same species of trees does in the arrangement of leaves or the form of blossom. That the physiological condition preceding this action should set the bird, and all kinds of birds, to the particular work of constructing nests, evidently requires some directive force supplemental to mere function, and the uniformities with which this works preclude the idea that each one is acting from an intelligent choice of either object or method. A hundred different species, of the same size, and surrounded by the same materials, and for which we might suppose the same sort of nest would answer, will build a hundred different kinds of nests; but a thousand birds of the same species, though widely separated, without instruction, some young, some old, will build exactly alike. The old show no more skill than the young; the young show no new ideas or independent methods. This uniformity within the limits of each species is best for the members of it. The variations, also, which mark the building of the different species, are found to be accurately adapted to the place and needs of each. Though the impulse works without comprehending its reasons, it works with the directive force of a wise and discriminating counsel. He who does not recognize the intelligence that rules it can scarcely himself be intelligent.

This constructive instinct is a large characteristic in the animal world. It appears wherever we look. The ants arrange their many-chambered and curious homes. The beaver constructs his strong dam, and builds his village of houses. The hornet builds its nest. The silk worm weaves its cocoon. The common caterpillar fills the forks of trees with hammocks. The spider beautifies the fields and fences with the entrance network of its dwellings. Animal life is everywhere exhibiting the activity of this adaptive process.

4. Many of the most wonderful instincts are for the *continuance of the species.* Some of these are so startlingly peculiar as to become impressive proofs of a distinct correlation of complex powers to specific ends—ends which lie outside of the common and necessary action of mere matter and life, and utterly beyond the reach of the animal's own knowledge and planning. This is illustrated in the building and feeding methods of the bees, already mentioned, and especially in the strange but effective process which they pursue in developing the queens. The modification of birds is but the beginning of the activity which the parental relation involves. The bird sits for weeks upon the eggs to hatch them—a service which, however plainly it is a means to an end, breaks abruptly across its usual habits, and forms a sort of specially inserted section in its life. After hatching, this same instinct not only defends the brood, by acts admirably

adapted to the object, but selects the proper food, and puts it into the mouth of the young. This order of things is pursued even when the parent had itself been artificially hatched and reared, and had no experience by which to learn.

Many varieties of insects are found depositing their eggs with the strictest regard to the presence of the food required by the young. This is attended with peculiarities which show that they do not understand the bearings of their action. The prospective adaptation not only crosses the chasm between the annual generations, but connects two states which have scarcely anything in common. The butterfly anticipates and provides for the food, not such as itself uses and enjoys, but such as the newly hatched larvae will need. "The tent moth lays her eggs upon the apple twig, closely packed and varnished to protect them till the warmth of spring wakes the young to life, when the new leaf is ready for their food. While forests of trees invite her by their slender twigs, on no tree does she put an egg but on the kind on which the larvæ may feed." "The *pompiles* at full age live on flowers, but their larvæ are carnivorous, and their mothers always provide for their nourishment by placing beside their eggs, in a nest prepared for the purpose, the bodies of some spiders or caterpillars."

Mr. Mivart mentions a certain wasp-like animal that, by stinging spiders in the particular part of the cephalothorax which contains the principal nervous center, paralyzes them without killing them, and in this condition stores them up to serve as food when the larvæ quit the egg. The mystery of the instinct is heightened by its leading the insect to sting the spider in precisely the right spot to produce the particular results required.

The unique fact of periodic migration is at least in some degree related to this purpose. Various birds make their way to the same nesting localities year after year over thousands of miles of land and sea, by day and by night. A common impulse is upon them, and hence they go in flocks, young and old alike. The impulse acts with the regularity of the budding of trees or the blooming of flowers. "Many fishes make long journeys to deposit their eggs in a place suitable for their young. The parent returns to the ocean, and the young fish when hatched and grown to proper size journeys to the great deep as well as if its parent had remained to act as guide. It is led to its right place as by a divine knowledge. The thousands that go out for the first time find their feeding grounds, and never forget to return when the time comes for them to deposit their spawn. Some seek the fresh streams, and some the salt ocean; each one seeks the proper condition for its young, which it is never to see, and to which it probably has no conscious relation. It leaves its accustomed haunts, where would seem to be the most natural place for breeding, and seeks out a far-distant location to which its instinct guides it. This impulse was given to complete its relation to the world, and is the same evidence of design as the form of the fin or the structure of the gill."

These few forms and examples of instinct will suffice to illustrate its nature and significance. It takes up the control or regulation of animal action at the point to which mere organization and function have brought it, and carries it up and over to the boundary at which intelligence and freedom come into play. The whole animal kingdom is astir with its action. Its utilities are omnipresent. It directs to a thousand specific objects needed in the whole system of things, with a uniformity on the one hand that looks like simple mechanics, and with an adaptiveness on the other hand that appears divinely wise and discriminating. It includes a principle of accommodating variability by which it rises far above a fixed automatism, and under stress of emergency presents the appearance of expedients full of inventive skill and adjustive purpose. The prescience and wisdom that work through it often far surpass the forecast and wisdom of man. When acting in normal conditions, undisturbed by disarranging circumstances, it never hesitates or falters, it takes no time for deliberation, and makes no mistakes. It works frequent prodigies which remain "insoluble problems" in speculative science, and justify the exclamation of Kant: "It is the voice of God." So impressively does it force its wonders of adaptive prevision and wisdom on the recognition of men, that when skeptical thought has excluded the rational theistic explanation of it all, atheistic speculation seeks some account of it in the supposition of an Unconscious Intelligence in the world itself. That it works for ends is the very essence or defining attribute of the power. So thoroughly and deeply is this its leading characteristic that descriptive science cannot describe its place and action except in the terms of final cause.

THE GENERAL CONSTITUTION OF THE WORLD

The matter bearing on the question of finality under this head is found in looking at the general relations between different parts of the earth-system itself, and the relation between this and other parts of the solar and starry systems.

1. The *history of the earth itself*, as clearly read in geological science, makes the fact indisputably certain that the progress of our globe has not been simply a forward and confused movement in time, but constantly toward what is better and more useful. It has been real advance. What each period was made by the preceding was not after the manner of a continuance on a level of miscellaneous and aimless uncertainty, but into a more elevated range of order and utility. The earliest and lowest geological condition was wholly unsuited to life. So far as discoverable, it was azoic. By some cause or other the atoms adopted action of beneficial tendency, and worked up into higher things than they first exhibited. In each later stage, there was an enriching harvest from the earlier. The movement steadily wrought out superior conditions. And as we stand in this *last age* and look back, we see an immense progression, wrought on the line of an orderly ascent through countless years, and we are surrounded with the products, delivered to us out of all that past, which provide for the existence and welfare of the human race. The movement has been from chaos to cosmos, or a world rich in orderly adaptations and in beauty. It has advanced from dead matter into life, and into suitable provision for that life. Metals and minerals have been formed and stored away, making possible the high utilities and enjoyments of the civilization and culture of this latest age of time. The history presents no appearance of aimlessness. The very law of progress, easily read in the earth's evolution, and sometimes urged by atheistic sophistry to discredit theism, is

really and in itself a fact of useful adaptation, incapable of explanation except in some original, fundamental, all-inclusive design.

2. The *existence and constitution of the atmosphere* reveal finality. The wisdom it displays cannot be credited to accident. It has been placed about our globe as an aerial ocean, of about forty-five miles depth. It is held down to the earth by the power of gravitation, with a force on the surface equal to about fifteen pounds to the square inch. It is composed of oxygen and nitrogen gases, in such proportions as to supply the conditions for life, both vegetable and animal. These elements are not united, but only mixed. Yet they are so balanced and held in equilibrium by the force of gravitation that they keep their relative proportions everywhere, while the particles have such easy motion among themselves as to permit us to move in the bottom of this atmospheric ocean without feeling its presence. "It is firm enough to support the wings of a lark as he mounts the sky, and yet so yielding as not to detain the tiniest insect in its flight." The atmosphere presents most impressive adaptations to the general constitution of the earth and all the utilities and enjoyments of the life of the world. A few of them will suffice as illustrations.

It bears and conveys whatever is needed for vegetable life and growth. The atmosphere meets the soil of the earth and joins with it in furnishing the conditions and productive forces for plant organization. If the soil holds and can give some portion, the air fits its own supply to that of the ground, and the mysterious process is accomplished in which nature rises above mechanical action into living forms. Not a seed germinates, not a flower blooms, not a tree grows, but as the atmosphere is present with its prepared materials and adapted forces. The treasures of the ground would be in vain if not supplemented in the air.

It is constituted into a medium for vision. This required a combination of special properties. One is transparency. Though the transparency of the atmosphere is not perfect, its actual degree of it is an essential thing in the adaptation of the world for such beings as are put here to inhabit it. But to complete the adaptation this property has been united with another—its diffusive power for the sun's rays. Else the light would pass right on, leaving vision really unprovided for. But every particle of the atmosphere, illuminated by direct ray of the sun, becomes itself a new centre of emission, radiating light in every direction. In this way the light is diffused and the whole atmosphere is illuminated. Thus is produced what we call daylight. When the sun's rays enter the upper air the whole mass becomes illuminated, and the landscape is brightened for the eye. A beam, entering a chamber, fills the whole space with light. "Were it not for the diffusive effect of the atmosphere on the sun's rays, the contrast between light and shadows would be so greatly increased that while objects directly illuminated by the sun would shine so brilliantly as to dazzle the eyes, all surrounding objects would be in darkness, and the interior of our dwelling would be as dark as night."

The atmosphere is adjusted to needful results on the world's temperature. Whatever may be the physical explanation of heat and its relation to light, whether or not both are only modes of motion and at bottom one, the effect is the same, and equally a necessary condition for the existence of organic life and for the comfort of sentient existences. "The atmosphere acts for diffusing heat just as it does for diffusing light. Were it not for this, the greatest extremes would be produced by the alternations of day and night, probably rendering the existence of the higher forms of organic life impossible on the globe. Not only does the atmosphere diffuse the heat of the sun's direct rays, and so mitigate the intensity with which these rays would smite, but it acts even more effectually for good in retaining on the surface the heat which the earth is constantly receiving. The atmosphere has been well compared to a mantle, enveloping the earth and protecting it from the chill of the celestial spaces through which we are rushing as the earth goes on in its orbit." In this ocean of air, diffusing and retaining the heat, we are kept warm. And by its incessant currents, produced by differing exposure to the sun's direct rays and by the earth's diurnal motion, the heat is carried and distributed over the globe in remoter zones and latitudes, making it more widely habitable, and breaking or preventing what would otherwise become unbearable extremes of climate.

3. The *existence of water, with its special physical constitution,* on the earth is a manifest adaptation to the same ruling utilities to which the other parts of the system look. Composed of two gases in union, with capacity for vaporization and condensation at fixed temperatures that are adjusted to the actual heat of the atmosphere, it plays a part in the aggregate world-economy, without which all other provision would prove abortive. Its addition to the world system makes actual all of the other great possibilities. Being given in the proportion it actually holds to other parts, and vaporizing and condensing at the point it does and must, it is carried by the atmosphere over the earth and supplied to the land in showers from the sky, and by ceaseless circuits from fountains to oceans and back again the continents are kept irrigated, and refreshment is furnished to all living existence. Nature's scheme of irrigation has always, indeed, awakened admiration and wonder. The peculiar constitution of water itself and the complex agencies employed in its distribution are full of clear evidences of beneficent counsel. Unquestionably they unite in serving the great ends which the other parts of nature make possible.

4. A singular and significant provision appears in *the law by which water expands below the freezing point.* This is exceptional. Generally bodies are expanded by heat and contracted by cold. Water itself follows this general law at all temperatures above 40°. As its surface becomes cooled, the chilled, and therefore heavier, portions sink toward the bottom, causing a circulation till the whole mass has sunk to 40°. From this point it becomes lighter by further cooling, and the cooled portion remains on top. At 32° it freezes. Prof. Cooke states the result: "Then comes into play still another provision in the properties of water. Most substances are heavier in their solid than in their liquid state; but ice, on the contrary, is lighter than water, and therefore floats on its surface. Moreover, as ice is a very poor conductor of heat, it serves as a protection to the lake, so that at the depth of a few feet, at most, the temperature of the water during winter is never under 40°, although the atmosphere may continue for weeks below zero. If water resembled other liquids, and continued to contract with cold to its freezing point—if this exception had not been made,

the whole order of nature would have been reversed. The circulation just described would continue until the whole mass of water in the lake had fallen to the freezing point. The ice would then first form at the bottom, and the congelation would continue until the whole lake had been changed into one mass of solid ice. Upon such a mass the hottest summer would produce but little effect; for the poor conducting power would then prevent its melting, and instead of ponds and lakes we should have large masses of ice, which during the summer would melt on the surface to a depth of only a few feet. It is unnecessary to state that this condition of things would be utterly inconsistent with the existence of aquatic plants or animals, and it would be almost as fatal to organic life everywhere; for not only are all parts of the creation so indissolubly bound together that if one member suffers all the other members suffer with it, but, moreover, the soil itself would, to a certain extent, share in the fate of the ponds. The soil is always more or less saturated with water, and, under existing conditions in our temperate zone, the frost does not penetrate to a sufficient depth to kill the roots and seeds of plants which are buried under it. But were water constituted like other liquids, the soil would remain frozen to the depth of many feet, and the only effect of the summer's heat would be to melt a few inches at the surface. It would be, perhaps, possible to cultivate some hardy annuals in such a climate, but this would be all. Trees and shrubs could not brave the severity of the winter. Thus, then, it appears that the very existence of life in these temperate regions of the earth depends on an apparent exception to a general law of nature, so slight and so limited in its extent that it can only be detected by the most refined scientific observation." This is exceedingly expressive of a purpose.

5. The *relations of organized bodies to their assigned place* exhibit remarkable correlations. The finality which appears in the inner order of organisms is carried further in the adaptation between them and the world without. Somehow or other both men and the lower animals have the benefit of a "pre-established harmony" provided between themselves and the place they come to occupy. This harmony is especially remarkable because the things found adjusted have their origins far apart and

independent. The earth existed long before man. When he came, it was necessary not only that his body should be internally organized, but externally adapted to conditions already existing. The two sides of his existence, the internal and the external, have been framed to each other with the finest accuracy. Outside of him, for instance, is material capable of affording nourishment. Within is an elaborate provision for utilizing that material. The soil, showers, and sunlight produce grains and fruits, and the digestive and nutritive systems are exactly arranged for using these products. The wheat in the field and the mill for making it into flour are not more clearly correspondent facts. Each of the senses answers to specific realities in external nature, and is answered to by them. The mind itself is correlated to the material world, and all its powers of knowledge stand face to face with objects to be known. In the need of sleep, man seems to be organized even to the movements of the solar system, the need of rest being met in the suitable conditions for it.

The various species of animals present even more striking adaptations to place and appointed modes of life. Man, by being rational and capable of clothing and sheltering himself, is cosmopolitan. The lower orders are more local and more distinctly adjusted to their limited ranges. Each order is found fundamentally organized for its element and place, in water, on land, or in the atmosphere. The fundamental structure is varied in endless diversities as situations are changed. All these variations from the ruling plan are not defects, but examples of the perfection of the adaptive law. When an experienced naturalist knows the situation, he can anticipate the organization, for it is found to follow the line of a rational accommodation. When he finds a particular, perhaps unique, feature of structure, he will look at once for its purpose, and expect to find some other reality to which it corresponds, marking the wisdom of the change.

These truths will be found exemplified in all grades of life, from animalculæ to mammoths. No ship on the sea is better fitted for its place than is the *nautilus pompylius*, that finds its water-tight compartments built in its little vessel by the very law of growth. No work of man can surpass the adaptation of the bird to the varied necessities and offices of life in the air—an equipped vessel for navigating the atmosphere. The earthworm gropes in the ground and finds full provision for its humble existence. The mole burrows in darkness through moisture and dirt, and comes out with its glossy fineness unsoiled. The walrus and the seal present forms of organization framed and compacted to the rigors of arctic cold and ice.

The fitting of animals to their place often involves peculiar provisions accommodating them to periodic changes of climate. In some cases this takes the astonishing form of hibernation—a falling, when winter approaches, into a peculiar and deep slumber, with very low vitality, in which condition they live off of their own stored-up substance, till spring calls to the awakening and to fresh growths of food. In other cases, nature thickens the coating of fur when the cold weather comes on, and thins it again when summer returns. These peculiar things cannot be fairly explained as mere results of the periodic change of temperature; for the facts, as well as some attendant and previsive instincts, anticipate the change and prepare for it. It arises from some profounder law or provision in the animal's system, whose machinery, it has been well said, "has been adjusted to the clockwork of the stars." However, the influence of environment in bringing about these adaptations is not, just here, the point of inquiry, but only whether in fact nature is found acting previsively for real ends. Such action, whatever solution of it may be offered, manifestly marks these arrangements in nature's work.

6. In the *relations of the earth to the solar system*, of which it forms a part, and of the solar system to the other parts of the stellar universe, we trace the reality of an adjusted order in grandest scale. Modern astronomy has opened the universe to view in proportions that awe and confound the human mind. The millions on millions of stars that fill the sky are now recognized as suns, probably surrounded, like our own, each by many circling worlds, system on system ranging away in space, one beyond another, with intervening distances compared with which the distance from the earth to the sun is but a span. The starry universe has grown to be virtually infinite to our view. But order illuminates it like light. Our earth, for instance, in size, weight,

figure, distance, orbital and axial motions, is fitted into the solar system in exactest conformity to the requirements of geometrical principles and the law of gravitation. The same is true of all the planets, with their satellites, in this system. In the precision of their revolutions under the two mighty forces by which their motion is determined, their ceaseless equipoise among themselves, their velocities both on axis and in orbit, their return in their mighty cycles being timed to very seconds, and in the amounts of light and heat furnished to them, they present an adjustment so complete and in such gigantic magnitudes as to kindle perpetual admiration and wonder. Astronomy finds the same law of order in each and all of the milliard stellar systems that have their place in infinite space, and in the relations which hold between them. Thus the universe, with its unnumbered groups of worlds, stretching into immensity, though a universe all in motion, is nevertheless an established and singing harmony.

It is impossible, in the small space allowed by the plan of this discussion, to present the particulars which exemplify these general statements. It would require the details of a full treatise on astronomy. For the specific and impressive facts the reader must be referred to works of that class.

CHEMISTRY

The point in chemistry bearing on the question of final cause is the evident constitution of the primitive *elements* for all the beneficent purposes of world-building and human welfare. When nature is examined to the last analysis of its matter, adaptation is a fact that refuses to disappear. The simple elements are discovered to be exactly fitted, not merely to produce *some* result by their chemical reactions, but precisely such results as serve to construct an orderly, habitable world, with provision for sentient enjoyment and human welfare. The properties found to belong to these elements mark them as prepared material. The adaptation of the sawed, planed, squared, and carved pieces of wood which the cabinet maker unites to make a table, or of the carefully shaped plates and bars and bolts and screws which the machinist forms into a steam engine, is only a faint suggestion of the wonderful adaptations which reveal themselves in the chemical elements.

To make this evident in a few illustrative examples, we cannot do better than to abridge some explanations from Prof. J. P. Cooke's *Religion and Chemistry*:

1. The great element of nature is oxygen. It forms one-fifth of the volume of the atmosphere. It composes between one-half and one-third of the crust of the globe. It makes up eight-ninths of all the earth's water, three-fourths of our bodies, not less than four-fifths of every plant, and at least one-half of the solid rocks. More than twenty tons of pressure to the square inch is required to reduce oxygen to a liquid condition. This will give some idea of the chemical force by which it is held imprisoned in its liquid and solid forms. In a tumbler of water there are no less than six cubic feet of oxygen gas, condensed to a liquid state and held there by the continuous action of a force which can be measured only by hundreds of tons of pressure. Who can estimate the silent chemical power by which this subtle material is fitted for building the solid and abiding foundations of the earth?

2. It can hardly be without a purpose that oxygen, as well as hydrogen, is entirely *destitute of both odor and taste*. As these gases exist in a free state, and only mixed in our atmosphere, these properties would become manifest if they existed. But if odor and taste were to be qualities concerned in the choice of foods and other discriminations by men and animals, this negative characteristic assumes the place of a fundamental condition. These discriminations would seem to be possible only in the absence of taste and odor in the essential gases.

3. The tendency of oxygen to *diffusion* is an important property. All gases tend to expand, and can be prevented from doing so only by being enclosed. Oxygen and nitrogen, the chief gases of the atmosphere, under this diffusive tendency, are so spread and mixed with each other over the whole earth that they are present in equal proportions everywhere. Analysis can detect no more than the slightest difference in composition between the air brought from the summit of the Alps and that from the deepest mine in Cornwall. Were it not for this law of diffusion,

this tendency to spread equally everywhere in spite of the presence of other gases, the two gases might separate partially, and the atmosphere would become unfitted for many of its most important functions. Take, for example, the function of transmitting sound. As the air is now constituted, there is a constancy of pitch, however far the sound travels. Any tone once generated remains the same tone till it dies away. Its degree of loudness alters in proportion to the distance of the listener, but the pitch is constant. Were it not, however, for this law of diffusion, were the atmosphere not perfectly homogeneous, and were the gases of which it consists even partially separated, there would have been a very different result. The constancy of pitch could no longer be depended upon. The sound, as it travelled, would vary with the ever varying medium through which it passed, and would arrive at the ear with a tone entirely different from that with which it started. Nor would it require any great difference in the medium to produce a sensible result, and to confuse all those delicate differences of pitch on which the whole art of music depends. Without this careful adjustment of force the magnificent creations of a Mozart or a Beethoven would be impossible.

4. Another property of oxygen must be mentioned—*that its temperature point for active union with other elements is fixed where it is.* In its common state in the air it is passive, inert. It seems devoid of any active properties. It is in contact with all matter; it bathes the most delicate animal organisms; it fills all the air passages of the lungs, and penetrates among the tissues. It seems wanting in all active or strong chemical force. But if the temperature be raised to red heat, what was lately so inert at once rushes into chemical union with other elements, the action exhibiting what we call fire. The gentle breeze which was waving the corn and fanning the browsing herds becomes the next moment a consuming fire, by which the works of man melt away into air. The transition from the inert to this active condition does not necessarily require the temperature of any large body of air, or of any combustible material to be raised to this high grade. There is a provision in nature by which the chemical combination, when once started, through sufficient heat at a

single point, is sustained till the whole is consumed. All combustion is a process of chemical combination. This is attended by the evolution of heat; and in the combination of oxygen with any substance enough heat is generated at the point of actual burning to continue it to the next part. Different substances ignite at different temperatures. Phosphorus, for instance, ignites at a temperature less than that of boiling water, sulphur at about 500°, wood at full red heat, anthracite coal at a white heat, while iron requires the highest heat of a blacksmith's forge. The point of ignition for different bodies being fixed, puts the energies of this powerful agent at the command of men. It is worthy of note that this point has been placed for wood, coal, and all common combustibles, sufficiently above the ordinary temperature of the air to insure general exemption from conflagration. Spontaneous combustion is thus provided against. And a check is put on the violence of burning, after combustion has been started. This is done by another provision—the energies of oxygen being tempered by extreme dilution. Experiments show that the slowness of combustion depends on the fact that in the atmosphere oxygen is mixed with a great mass of inert gas, and the proportion has been so adjusted in the scheme of creation as generally to restrain the awakened energies of the fire element within narrow limits, which man appoints. It is easy to see how a small change in the amount of oxygen in the air would involve all organized matter in a general conflagration.

Now this property of oxygen, in connection with its fixed relative amount, prepares it for all the beneficent uses it serves, not only in its passive, quiet state, but in its active energies, giving so-called "fire" to man, essential both to common daily life and to all the industries, sciences, arts, and culture by which the race rises into dignity and power. Fire is one of the most valuable servants of mankind; it is the great source of artificial heat and light. In the steam engine it is the apparent origin of that power which animates the commerce and the industry of the civilized world. Under its influence iron becomes plastic; the ores give up their metallic treasures. It is the agent of all the arts. In the light of modern science all this utility comes from the peculiar capacities of oxygen. The adaptations are too striking to be overlooked, and too elaborate and adjusted to be counted only *happenings*. Immeasurable power is found locked up in perfect mildness, and submitted to the service of man. This strongest of the chemical elements, although a permanent gas, forms more than one-half of the solid crust of the earth, and is endowed with such mighty affinities that it is retained securely by them in its solid state, yet it is, in the atmosphere, so shorn of its energies as not to singe the down of the gossamer, and still so tempered that its powers may be evoked at the will of man and made subservient to his wants.

5. When oxygen unites with the elements of wood, coal, or other combustible matter, two chief products are set free: carbonic dioxide gas and aqueous vapor. These products are colorless and transparent, without odor or taste. They escape from the burning wood, ascend the chimney, and pass off into the general atmosphere. If the chemist takes the smoke and weighs it, he finds that it weighs more than the burnt wood—a weight equal to that of the wood and of the air consumed in the burning. Now, provision is made in nature by which this smoke is worked up again into new combinations. A new cycle of changes is begun where the flame ends. The carbonic dioxide and the aqueous vapor, after roving at liberty for awhile, are absorbed by the leaves of trees and the blades of grass, and under the influence of the sun-rays, help to form new wood and grow crops for the use of man. Everything appears to be ordered so as to run in channels of economic utility. The atmosphere is kept pure, nothing is lost, and nature keeps up a beneficent order.

6. The original adaptation of oxygen for world-building is strikingly shown by the largeness of its office in forming the body of the earth. We must look at it not only in its place and relations in the atmosphere, fitting it as the medium for life and breathing, and furnishing fire and all its dependent utilities of heat and combustion, but in producing materials for building our globe. In its earlier stages, at least, the making of the world seems to have been a process of burning, and its foundations were laid in flames. Examining the matter of which the earth is made, we find a great many substances, all composed of about seventy so-called chemical elements; that is, substances considered as simple,

because not yet, at least, found capable of being decomposed. Accepting oxygen as the supporter of combustion, the great mass of the remaining elements are combustible; that is, under certain conditions they combine rapidly with oxygen, evolving light and heat. Carbon is an element, phosphorus is an element; so is iron, sulphur, and each of the other metals. Out of these, combined with oxygen, the world is built, oxygen being the largest element. Oxygen unites with calcium, forming lime, and lime rocks, under various modifications, constitute a large part of the earth's crust. It unites with silicon, forming silica, the very hard white solid appearing in the varieties of stone known as quartz, rock crystal, agate, jasper, chalcedony, opal, and others. Over one-half of the weight of each of these is oxygen. In union with aluminum it forms a compound called alumina, a substance out of which nature makes sapphires and rubies, and which, when united with silica and water, furnishes us with clay. With magnesium it forms magnesia, and this in union with silica makes, according to the proportions, hornblende or augite, two minerals which abound in many varieties of rock. Add water to the composition, and we get also serpentine or soapstone, with many other allied mineral species. Potassum with oxygen turns to potash. Melt potash, lime, and silicious earth together, and we have glass. Unite potash, silica, and alumina, and we get feldspar; combine them in different proportions, and we have mica; in other proportions, garnet. Lastly, mix quartz and feldspar together with mica or hornblende, in an indiscriminate jumble, and we have the several varieties of the granite rock. Thus by union of oxygen with a few other elements, under what is known as the process of burning, the materials are formed which, by further combinations, produce all the varieties of the earth's rocks and soils. More than one-half of the whole consists of oxygen. Silicon forms about one-fourth. Other elements enter in smaller proportions. Evidently, therefore, so far as our knowledge extends, oxygen, silicon, carbon, together with a few metals, have been the chief building materials in making the world, and oxygen has been, so to speak, the universal cement by which the various elements have been bound together in the grand and diversified whole.

We might go on to collect from reliable chemical authorities hundreds of such examples, showing adaptation in the elementary matter of the world. The properties of hydrogen are only less significant than those of oxygen. Facts of definite utility for world structure come into view all through the work of chemistry. They fill the mind with wonder, and many of them read like romance when Science in her soberest moods sets them before us. Especially is this so when molecular physics, by means of the spectrum, shows the elements to be the same in distant worlds and on the earth, whether procured from water or coal of our planet or from meteoric iron, whether in the light of a lamp or coming from the sun or Sirius or Arcturus, making it thus exceedingly probable that the molecules have had a common origin.

We mention, however, only one thing more, especially deserving of notice both because it is fundamental in the whole system of chemistry, and because of its bearing on the point which we wish to emphasize. This is the "law of definite proportions," or equivalents, in the union of the various elements in chemical reactions. When any two of these elements unite to form a compound body, the proportions in which they combine are not decided by chance. We cannot unite them in any proportions we may please. They are fixed in each case according to an unvarying law; and the relative amount required seems to be weighed out by nature in her delicate scales with an exactness which no art can attain. Works on chemistry usually give tables showing the numerical value or "atomic weight" for each element. Whenever the elements unite with each other, it is found to be in the exact proportions indicated by these numbers, or else in some multiple of these proportions. These values are called "atomic weights," because according to the theory of modern chemistry they represent the relative weights of the ultimate atoms of the elements. If this be the case, it is evident that when the atoms group themselves together to form the molecules of various substances, the elements must combine by whole atoms. The law of proportions, therefore, seems to point back to definite and unvarying properties in the assumed atoms themselves, by which they are adapted to produce what we call the elements, or, rather, the molecules of which these elements consist.

The adaptive existence and action thus begin not only back of organisms and chemical compounds, but back of the elements themselves. The very atoms contain the law. The principle of finality acts from the beginning. The elementary molecules are the ultimate things that science can directly examine in its retrogressive analysis, and thus this testimony of chemistry as to the marks of adaptation which they show is of exceeding value. Science will hardly be able to eliminate from nature what is found inhering in the molecules. Prof. Cooke, from whose able work we have drawn most of the facts recited on this point, well concludes: "The great argument of Natural Theology rests on a basis which no present theories of development can touch. I have endeavored to show that there is abundant evidence of design even in the properties of the chemical elements, the stones of nature's edifice. The footprints of the Creator are nowhere more plainly visible than on that very matter which the materialists so vainly worship." It is not Prof. Cooke alone who assures us of this fact. He is simply one in the line of competent witnesses to it. Probably no philosopher of recent times was better acquainted with the interior realities of nature than Sir John Herschel, and he has put his testimony concerning these elementary molecules in the striking and memorable declaration that they possessed all the characteristics of "manufactured articles." Prof. J. Clerk Maxwell, an authority second to none in experimental physics, is led by his minute research to the same conclusion: "It is well known that living beings may be grouped into a certain number of species, defined with more or less precision, and that it is difficult or impossible to find a series of individuals forming the links of a continuous chain between one species and another. In the case of living beings, however, the generation of individuals is always going on, each individual differing more or less from its parents. Each individual, during its whole life, is undergoing modification, and it either survives and propagates its species, or dies early, according as it is more or less adapted to the circumstances of its environment. Hence, it has been found possible to frame a theory of the distribution of organisms into species by means of generation, variation, and discriminative destruction. But a theory of evolution of this kind cannot be applied to the case of molecules, for the individual molecules neither are born nor die, they have neither parents nor offspring, and so far from being modified by their environment, we find that two molecules of the same kind, say of hydrogen, have the same properties, though one has been compounded with carbon and buried in the earth as coal for untold ages, while the other has been 'occluded' in the iron of a meteorite, and after unknown wanderings in the heavens has at last fallen into the hands of some terrestrial chemist. The process by which the molecules become distributed into distinct species is not one of which we know any instances going on at present, or of which we have as yet been able to form any mental representation. If we suppose that the molecules known to us are built up each of some moderate number of atoms, these atoms being all of them exactly alike, then we may attribute the limited number of molecular species to the limited number of ways in which the primitive atoms may be combined so as to form a permanent system. But though this hypothesis gets rid of the difficulty of accounting for the independent origin of different species of molecules, it merely transfers the difficulty from the known molecules to the primitive atoms. How did the atoms come to be all alike in those properties which are in themselves capable of assuming any value?... We have seen that the very different circumstances in which different molecules of the same kind have been placed have not, even in the course of many ages, produced any appreciable difference in the value of these constants. If, then, the various processes of nature to which these molecules have been subjected since the world began have not been able in all that time to produce any appreciable difference between the constants of one molecule and those of another, we are forced to conclude that it is not to the operation of any of these processes that the uniformity of the constant is due. The formation of the molecule is, therefore, an event not belonging to that order of nature under which we live. It is an operation of a kind which is not, so far as we are aware, going on in the earth or in the sun or the stars, either now or since these bodies began to be formed. It must be referred to the epoch, not of the formation of the earth or of the solar system, but of the establishment of the existing order of nature, and till not only these worlds and systems, but the very order of nature itself is dissolved, we have no reason to expect the occurrence of any operation of a similar kind.... Whether or not the conception of a multitude of beings existing from all eternity is in itself self-contradictory, the conception becomes palpably absurd when we attribute a relation of quantitative equality to all these beings. We are then forced to look beyond them to some common cause or common origin to explain why this singular relation of equality exists, rather than any one of the infinite number of possible relations of inequality.

"Science is incompetent to reason upon the creation of matter itself out of nothing. We have reached the utmost limit of our thinking faculties when we have admitted that, because matter cannot be eternal and self-existent, it must have been created. It is only when we contemplate not matter in itself, but the form in which it actually exists, that our mind finds something on which it can lay hold. That matter, as such, should have certain fundamental properties, that it should have a continuous existence in space and time; that all action should be between two portions of matter, and so on, are truths which may, for aught we know, be of the kind which metaphysicians call necessary. We may use our knowledge of such truths for purposes of deduction, but we have no data for speculating on their origin.

"But the equality of the constants of the molecules is a fact of a very different order. It arises from a particular distribution of matter, a *collocation*, to use the expression of Dr. Chalmers, of things which we have no difficulty in imagining to have been arranged otherwise. But many of the ordinary instances of collocation are adjustments of constants, which are not only arbitrary in their own nature, but in which variations actually occur; and when it is pointed out that these adjustments are beneficial to living beings, and are therefore instances of benevolent design, it is replied that those variations which are not conducive to the growth and multiplication of living beings tend to their destruction, and to the removal thereby of the evidence of any adjustment not beneficial. The constitution of an atom, however, is such as to render it, so far as we can judge, independent of all the dangers arising from the struggle for existence. Plausible reasons may, no doubt, be assigned for believing that if the constants had varied from atom to atom through any sensible range, the bodies formed by aggregates of such atoms would not have been so well fitted for the construction of the world as the bodies which actually exist. But as we have no experience of bodies formed of such variable atoms this must remain a bare conjecture.

"Atoms have been compared by Sir J. Herschel to manufactured articles, on account of their uniformity. The uniformity of manufactured articles may be traced to very different motives on the part of the manufacturer.... There are three kinds of usefulness in manufactured articles: cheapness, serviceableness, and quantitative accuracy. Which of these was present to the mind of Sir J. Herschel we cannot now positively affirm, but it was at least as likely to have been the last as the first, though it seems more probable that he meant to assert that a number of exactly similar things cannot be each of them eternal and self-existent, and must therefore have been made, and that he used the phrase 'manufactured article 'to suggest the idea of their being made in great numbers."

LIFE

The term "life" is a name given to an unknown force productive of well-known and unquestionable phenomena. What it is *per se* we know not. It is something different from everything not designated by the term itself. Between living and dead matter there is a chasm across which science has as yet shown no bridge. It has found no life not originating from previous life. Spontaneous generation is as yet unknown.

The force we call life has several clear and peculiar characteristics. One is its superiority to mere mechanism. It is itself the force which determines the mechanical relations and combinations of atoms, molecules, cells, and tissues, resulting in organs and organisms with their functions. The life force, whatever it is, works with the elementary particles, arranging them, accumulating them, and evolving them in what we call growth. It is allowable, indeed, if the mechanical view of nature is to furnish our terminology, to call these combinations "mechanical," as the result of molecular collocations and interactions, or modes of motion. But all attempted explanations of life as mere mechanism are radically vicious by treating mechanism as the cause of itself, or in other words, shutting out of view the necessary demands of the law of causation. Life creates organs for itself, transforming amorphous masses into veritable constructions, of skilful coordination and adaptation. It *uses* the principle of mechanism and subordinates it to its own ends.

Another characteristic is its control of the simply chemical forces. The nature of chemical affinity has been made evident in treating of the combinations of oxygen with other elements. That force plainly falls short of what is known as vitality, or life. No mere chemical interaction has ever been known to produce life or result in it. Life does not act according to chemical formulæ, but crosses them, and bends to its own uses the energies which these formulæ measure. This force seizes the chemical elements and directs them in lines of movement not only impossible to chemical action, but reversing it. It builds up organisms and keeps them in action according to its own laws. When, however, the vital force ceases, the chemical forces come again into ruling sway, and pull down what life built up. They attack the dead body or tree and reduce it to dust. The organic being struggles for existence, and lives only because the vital principle holds the physical forces in abeyance and makes them sources of support. In a certain sense it is the physical forces that build up all organic structures. Atheistic scientists are never done telling us this. But these physical forces serve this purpose only because, for the time, they are dominated by a superior force. The moment vitality is gone they tear down the body which they were made to construct. In no just sense can the chemical forces, any more than the mechanical, be held to be the same as the vital, as they thus stand, in some degree, at least, in antagonistic relation. In the decay of wood and of animal matter the chemical process, in reality, is the same as burning—an oxidation of the substances. When the albuminous matter is large, as in animals, the decay goes on rapidly. "Life, during its whole existence, is an untiring builder, repairing the waste of the body; the oxygen of the atmosphere is a fell destroyer." When at last the builder ceases, the chemical forces, acting alone, crumble the organism into dust. This life force is the latest born, so far as, from the geologic pages, we can read the birth periods of the forces that appear in nature, and the time may come when it may vanish from our globe and leave the chemical and physical forces victor on the field. But for the present, it exists as a superior form of force, irreducible to the terms of any other, and unaccountable by mere evolution of the physical and chemical forces.

Final cause is unquestionable in the actings of this force. Though life appears in an innumerable variety of forms, wherever found it moves with discriminative precision to distinct and determinate ends under laws operating from the initial or causal point. Each distinguishable species exhibits its own kind in continuous succession, showing an adjusted and fixed constitution. However alike the initial form of different species may look at the start, or in inchoate stages, the line of movement never falls into confusion, or issues in a species not its own. The goal of the evolution, even in the feeblest germs, is so firmly predetermined as to bend to its own purpose the encountered action of all the lower forces. It is true, that it is only after life has issued in a well-defined organism, that the end becomes clearly perceptible and impressive to the observer. In amorphous aggregations of living "protoplasm," or the lowest forms of organization, and in the simple cells and tissues of the earliest stages of growth in even the most highly organized species, the secret of the wonderful adaptation, with its provided differentiation into the minutest features of the parent species, is not yet disclosed. But when the initial cells and forming tissues are unfolded into organs, and these correlated into complete beings, then it becomes impressively sure that the germs were not fortuitous complications, but carried from the start a purpose enstamped on their life force and molecular structure. The potency and law of all that comes out of them must be in them from their beginning—a distinct correlation to future, discriminated, and intelligent ends.

A few illustrations will suffice to explain and certify this fact. Take, for instance, the egg of a bird. Its contents present only a yolk surrounded by the albumen, or white. To the unaided eye they appear only as two homogeneous semi-fluid masses of matter. The microscope reveals but little more. At best it discloses no trace of organs, or anything suggestive of the articulated structure into which it is to be formed. But when the egg is subjected, for a certain time, to the proper degree of warmth, either by the brooding of the mother bird or by artificial heat, there comes forth from that egg a bird perfect in all its parts. The life force, whatever it may be, as an artificer, proceeding on a plan of rational and systematic coordination of means to ends, and of beginnings to specialized results, has not only marshalled the molecules and constructed a bony framework and organs of circulation, digestion, respiration, of sight, hearing, taste, and smell, and manufactured, of suitable tissues, muscles and nerves of sensation and motion, but has united all these organs and parts, with their respective functions, into a symmetrically formed living bird. The process may be watched from day to day, and from hour to hour, and every step may be traced from the earliest segregation of the yolk, and the faint outline of a living form up to the completion of the work. That the result is already determined in the initial life of the egg is evident from the adaptive forecast with which the force in the egg of each species selects its appropriate form of structure out of numberless possible ones, and from the discriminated uniformity and certainty with which it shapes all the material into that form. For there are many species or kinds of life, distinguished by characteristics that run through their whole existence and rule in the process which forms each individual. Though the contents of a hundred different kinds of eggs present to the eye of science no perceptible difference in substance or composition, yet the life germ of each builds after its own kind. That of the eagle builds only an eagle. That of the robin constructs a robin. In every case the end is determined at the beginning, and the provision seeks and effects the reproduction of the specific form through a long eclectic process that adjusts with the finest precision every bone and organ and muscle and nerve and feather of the complex organism to the predetermined model required by the interests of the animal.

As another instance, we may take an acorn dropped from the oak. The question is: Does it reveal a real provision for an end? The acorn looks like only a little dull matter, but the law for the oak of a century's subsequent growth is written effectively in its life force and organization. It contains a distinct provision for a purpose already fixed and measured. Placed under right conditions of soil, moisture, and heat, it proceeds to show the design wrapped up and hidden in its living and wisely adapted germ. It is potentially all that comes out of it. Over against all confusing forces of nature and man, roots and trunk and boughs and branches have all been settled in the acorn as certainly as the keeping of time is settled in the structure of a watch, or the scanning of the heavens has been provided for in the make-up of the telescope. In all the manifold kinds of plant life each seed is predetermined for the product after its kind. Though the seed is so small as to be almost microscopic, the life presses right on across the direction of all known chemistries. It takes up the physical forces, and bends and utilizes them to a distinct result far above the possibilities of dead matter.

There is a further fact included here, of very clear and positive significance—the production of the seed itself. It must strike every thoughtful mind as a wonderful fact, that, in addition to this development from seeds, the life-processes in every tree and flower, and indeed in all organic nature, go right on and prepare seed for future growths, year after year. This is a distinct and striking pre-arrangement for the future. We know of no *a priori* necessity in the nature of atoms or molecules, or of living matter, why the dying plant or tree should provide a specialized structure for beginning another, or why the vegetation of one summer should take account for vegetation in the next. That it does so, however, is the very fact of nature's order. And the wisdom of the order is as clear as is its adaptive relation of means to ends.

The whole realm of organic nature teems with the industries of this life force. The earth is the theatre of their crowded activity. They are omnipresent and ceaseless. They move forward in countless lines of systematic productive work. They are adjusted to an intelligent order, and to rational and benevolent ends. They clothe the ground with the green and glory of millions of plants and flowers and useful products. They manufacture food for the myriads of sentient creatures that fill the earth and air. Could our ears catch the sound, they would be filled with the din of the countless and incessant processes, selecting the chemical elements from the air and water, pumping the saps up the veins, and elaborating the appropriate tissues of wood and leaf and flower and seed. In a higher range the life force populates the earth with animals possessed of organizations adapted to their place and prepared for an existence of enjoyment. In this force the system of nature is carried forward and upward into the higher grades which exhibit ends worthy of the grand preparation in the long development of the in-organic realm. The advent of life, with its clear acting for ends, reveals final cause for all that preceded it, and that would otherwise have failed to suggest the relation. Life makes all nature luminous with purposive action. In myriad ways and modes it is found correlated, not only to continuance of existence, but to the interests of beings capable of enjoyment and happiness. So impressive is the intelligence with which its force is made to act, so rich in wise adaptations are the products of its industry, so multiplied are its omnipresent wonders, that the observant mind has always and everywhere recognized it as carrying on and accomplishing real purposes; and the forms of speech in every land have been shaped to this truth. It is not to be wondered at that when Von Hartmann starts out with an atheistic view of the world, he must, in writing a philosophy of "the Unconscious," smuggle in some conception of intelligence under this contradictory term, in order to meet the necessity, still forced on the reason, of postulating some intelligent cause for these irreducible facts of finality. Rudolf Schmid well says: "One of the most remarkable philosophic testimonies for the right of teleology is the philosophic system of Eduard Von Hartmann, who, although he calls his absolute the Unconscious, ascribes to it an unconscious intelligence and an unconscious will, and makes the observation and acknowledgment of designs and ends, which he sees in the whole realm of the world of phenomena, an essential part of his entire system."

It is to be distinctly observed that this conclusion is not dependent on any particular theory of life. Whether life be held to be a result of organization, or itself the organizing energy—as it certainly shows itself to be in its actual processes and work—will make no difference. Should the extremest suggestion offered by the "mechanical theory" of nature be taken as scientific truth, that what we call life is due to a special mode of motion or an inter-relation of atoms or molecules, and that there is really no essential difference between the so-called living and dead worlds, the facts of life would still remain the same, so far as finality is concerned. Should it be explained—though at present there is no prospect of its being so explained—from the mere mechanism of atoms, still the special determination, by its action, of atomic, molecular, and cellular structures to millions of distinct and self-perpetuating forms of organization, in which complex parts are rationally correlated to each other and to useful and beneficent ends, remains a fact. Out of a few simple elements this inscrutable force forms the whole world of organized existences in such clear subjection to orderly thought that orderly thought easily traces it out and exhibits it in the wonderful classifications of scientific systems. Final cause is not refuted by calling the force "mechanical," especially so in view of the fact that the very conception of mechanism is primarily formed from the processes of human industry in which intention controls. The very roots of the concept "mechanical" stand in, as they arose out of, teleological soil. Indeed, man knows of no reality which he can positively affirm to be outside of all relation of means and ends and undetermined by this relation, from which to form a concept of mechanism that shall positively bar out finality. As we know mechanism, it is the product of design, however destitute of conscious intelligence itself may be. And so, even a mechanical explanation of life is no disproof of design, and the proper proofs of finality in it would remain unimpaired.

MIND

In psychology, in which we reach the highest point in the study of finite existences, we reach also the most unquestionable facts of finality. Should men deny final causes in each and all of the phenomena of creation below this, they cannot deny it here. For besides the indubitable adaptations in the different powers of the human mind to one another and all their great functions connecting its existence with the outer world, there is a conscious actual exercise of final cause by men every day and hour of their waking lives. Working with aims is the great characteristic of the mental world. There are three classes of facts to be noticed in this relation.

1. *Mind is always acting with consciousness of purposes.* The grandest fact in human consciousness, in daily life, in the world's history, is intentional action, pursuit and accomplishment of ends. Whatever explanation may be made of the nature of mind, whether considered a different entity from matter, as all the evidence shows it to be, or looked upon, in materialistic view, as only a resultant of material organization, two facts remain. *First*, that the mind is a *begun* existence. Thus its existence comes under the law of causation, and all that is in it and all that its action exhibits must be referred to an adequate producing cause. *Secondly*, that the mind itself acts as a final cause, exhibiting phenomena in which means are used for predetermined ends. If, therefore, on the one hand, mind is, as we have every reason to believe it to be, a different entity from matter, we are face to face with the fact of an originated existence or agent actually set, somehow, by its cause, to the function of acting for ends. If, on the other hand, we should for argument's sake consent to the materialist's assertion that what we call mind is a mere product or manifestation of organized molecules, then right here at the summit of nature, nature pure and simple is acting for ends. For, of this acting in fact every man is conscious. The effect of the materialist's scheme, in destroying the substantial difference between mind and matter and abolishing freedom, is to reduce mind to mere physics. It thus throws all the purposive action of man into the domain of simple nature. It cannot, however, deny

the reality of such purposive action, without denying the witness of consciousness, and so overthrowing the foundations of all knowledge. Thus, in either case, we have in the human mind an originated or begun existence, an existence belonging to the great aggregate of nature, that exhibits the reality of the action of final cause in the world.

In view of these facts one is amazed at the fatuity of the Positive Philosophy, and of those who have fallen into its shallow absurdity of undertaking to affirm that final cause can nowhere be found, and the search after it is illusory. Mr. J. S. Mill tells us that final causes are "unknown and inscrutable." Prof. Huxley joins in denouncing "the fruitless search after final causes" and "those hardy teleologists who are ready to break through all the laws of physics in chase of their favorite will-o-the-wisp." It is strange indeed that this materialistic philosophy, which seeks to wipe out the distinction between mind and matter, has been unable to find what every man is conscious of every day and hour of his waking life. Every sane person is thoroughly aware that, with a few insignificant exceptions due to weariness or caprice, he never acts, in either great or trifling affairs, without definitely formed purposes. He is always seeking ends. He would take it as an insult to be charged with living or acting below the rational grade. Even in writing denials of final cause, men are exhibiting its action. They act teleologically while they are writing down teleology.

Probably, however, only anti-teleologists of the extreme materialistic school mean to deny real final cause in the activity of our minds, counting it an illusive resultant of the mechanism of molecules. Others admit that man forms and accomplishes real purposes, and that the products of the whole world of human industry are products of design. They deny design only for the products of nature, as distinguished from the products of man's industry. They find in the universe no pursuit of ends but that of which man is the author. And they seem to assume that for the acting for ends of which man is conscious, and for all the results of this action, we need not go back of the human mind itself—that we may look upon the mind as the sole and absolute author of this kind of activity, and that somehow or other it is all explained in man's own personality and freedom. But to show the utter insufficiency of this explanation, and to prove that the admission of human design requires the admission of more, it is enough to recall the fact that man himself, being an originated being, this capacity or function of his mind is itself an adaptation to ends. All the adaptations that he originates are potentially included and provided for in the powers and faculties of his mental constitution. His conscious action as a final cause, and the necessity so to act, are simply two sides of one great reality in his psychical life. Not only is action for ends by men the most imposing and imperial fact in the world, filling the earth with the tremendous energies which form civilizations and make histories, but it is a necessity which arises out of this very constitution given to mind. This necessity is in no way contradictory to man's real freedom. For although he possesses freedom, yet his freedom consists only in choosing *among* ends, not in any possibility of acting without ends. It is impossible for man to escape the law of this kind of action. If he even attempts to refuse to pursue ends, his very attempt is the action and exhibition of a purpose. The mind is not only adapted to act for finality, but finality is the very law of its constitution. It is not only a *possibility* of his freedom, but a necessity in his freedom. The constitution of the mind, therefore, itself embodies the principle and fact of finality. As nature here compels action for ends, all such action belongs to nature's constitution.

2. The wonderful *adaptation of the mind's powers to one another in the unity of its conscious existence, and of each and all to the aggregate life to which man's bodily organization fits him,* has always arrested the interest and awakened the admiration of thoughtful students of psychology. In the great fundamental powers of the mind, for instance, known as *"the intellect" "the sensibility,"* and *"the will,"* in which, in orderly dependent capacity, we *know, we feel,* we *will,* there is a clear adjustment to the end of constituting an intelligent, self-determining personal being. In this organization of powers in the unity of a psychical existence, there is created the highest form of finite being of which we have any conception. There can be no question that these great powers, intellect, sensibility, and will, rise one above

another in adaptations marvelously fitted to each other, and with functions all looking forward to the great end of personality. The finest adaptations in physical structures are coarse and bungling compared with the fineness of the correlation of these powers.

In the subdivisions, also, of the intellectual power, the sense-perception, the memory and imagination, the faculties of discursive and intuitional thought, the same principle of adaptive order holds. Each faculty presents in itself a wonderful provision for a function useful to man; and their adjustment to each other, in relations of interdependence and cooperation, taking up and completing each other's processes and products in rational results, carry up the human constitution to the high rank of an intelligent, self-determining, moral being. Is it possible to look upon this personality, with its harmony and consistency of co-acting powers, as the result of chance? Or upon this intelligence as the product of non-intelligent forces? Or upon this liberty as the development of necessity? Is the constitution of mind, whose imperial characteristic is to act for ends, itself void of a provided adaptation to the great function it actually fulfils? The fact cannot be rationally thus viewed. Rather, all the mind's powers reveal themselves, in actual consciousness, as being themselves predetermined for the exhibition of that great function.

But the mental constitution is suited also to the capacities of the *bodily organization*. This is a truth of pro-founder significance than is generally recognized. The physical organism is just such as the mind's faculties require to give them full play and exercise. The human mind and body are plainly for each other. It is a shallow misconception that represents matter as intrinsically evil and the body as a clog or prison unsuited to the soul's powers. So accurately does man's own body—not that of an animal—answer the soul's needs as an instrument in every organ and fiber, that it looks as if the soul had organized and molded it all to its own wants and capabilities. The bodily distinctions of man as separating him from the rest of the animal world, are found to correspond in exactest degree to the mental distinctions that separate him from them. If man is a personality, with an outlook, in free intelligence, into possibilities beyond mere animal life, his body is just as clearly an organ of such personality. If the human mind were furnished with only an animal's body, even that of the anthropoid apes, said to be so similar to man's organization, such body would indeed be a hindrance, an incapacitating bondage, nullifying the mind's powers and reducing them to helplessness. For instance, with only an ape's hind feet for feet, and an ape's fore feet for hands, the human mind would be helpless before all the great tasks of life, its mechanical industries would be impossible, civilizations would be swept away, and the scientific faculties buried as in a tomb. The mind's faculties would have no adequate instruments with which to move forth into developed power and fruits. On the other hand, were an animal, even the highest below man, furnished with a man's mind, the gift would be worse than in vain. But man's nature presents no such unadjusted conjunction of mental and physical constitutions, in which the bodily organ is a useless instrument, or the mind a mighty and grand capacity disabled and made prisoner in an unfit structure. It presents the happy adaptation in which mind and its organ are manifestly made for each other. The aggregate life for which man's bodily organization prepares him is just the life which the mind's lofty capacities and powers can employ, utilize, and bring into full fruitage of good.

3. The *laws of pure thought, i.e.,* the established and necessary modes and products of our rational faculties, *are found to tally, in most impressive accuracy, with the realities found in the universe around us.* Truth, as found in the mind's own action, is found to be truth in the great cosmos without. Thus our knowledge is real knowledge. For it is of the very essence of knowledge that it knows a reality. Otherwise it is not knowledge. And the point to be noticed is that our pure thought-processes, starting from the phenomena of experience, but going far beyond them, guided by the intuitions of the reason, reach necessary conclusions which are found to express, not fictions, but great realities long before actualized in the plan and facts of the universe.

To explain this a few facts in psychology must be recalled: (1) The mind gains its earliest knowledge through the powers of sense-perception and consciousness. These furnish a knowledge of material things and of psychical acts. (2) By the power of representation, in which the mind recalls and reknows the objects of presentative knowledge, in the forms of memory and imagination, it accumulates and commands its acquisitions of empirical knowledge for the use of the thought-power. (3) The powers of thought now proceed, through acts of judgment, analysis, comparison, and synthesis, to form concepts or general notions. In these the relations of material and psychical phenomena are generalized in forms of thought. Guided by certain *a priori* relations and principles, intuitively evident, such as the relations of sub-stance and attribute, cause and effect, time and space, means and end, the thought-power develops the logical processes of inductive and deductive reasoning. It determines the laws of logic, which, indeed, are but the fixed and necessary principles and processes of thinking. Especially out of the time and space relations, this power develops the mathematical concepts of number and magnitude and the axioms and truths of mathematical reasoning and conclusion. Under its own necessary and universal laws thought thus constructs the entire science of pure mathematics. It determines relations that are necessarily and forever true in pure thought. It is in the applications of mathematical truth to the facts of the physical universe that the adaptations in the constitution of the mind become most conspicuously manifest.

To a full understanding of this a few other things must be remembered. *First*, that the idea of number, which, along with symmetry, is inherent in the mind, is developed, not from without, but from within. It arises when in consciousness we are aware of psychical acts or states of greater or less continuance, in connection with the continuing identity of the ego as the conscious agent, the succession or repetition of these psychical acts becoming the occasion of the idea of time as their necessary condition. Occurring once, twice, or oftener, they introduce the conception of number, out of which, as a time-relation, all arithmetical and algebraic mathematics are developed. These, therefore, are a product of the mind's own creative power, under its own subjective and necessary laws of thought. "Pure arithmetic and algebra deal only with ideal concepts conditioned on ideal time." Though developed on *occasion* of experience, their results go far beyond experience, and stand for truths which the human mind determines must hold everywhere and forever. *Secondly,* the whole science of geometrical quantities and relations is equally a product of the mind. Geometry is not the science of the relations of space, but of the relations *conceived possible in space.* It assumes pure space in which it places its ideal creations. The geometrical concepts are all idealized. For example, the mathematical "point," the mathematical "line," the mathematical "surface," are never known as physical realities. They are not things seen or imaged. The point, as position without extension, or the line, without breadth or thickness, is not known to our senses. The point is a zero of magnitude—yet it is not nothing. "Nothing is nowhere, but the point is somewhere." The mind, starting from experiences of extended material objects, goes beyond experience and creates these concepts as the starting points for true reasoning, or the beginnings of thought-processes, through which are built up coherent and far-reaching systems of ideal truth. With these beginnings, *the point, the line, the surface, the triangle,* and *solid,* and the axioms of pure thought, the mind goes into space or vacancy, and determines, among motions, divisions, and relations conceivable in it, what must be ideally and forever true of them. It thus forms a science of the possible and necessary relations of existences in space. It is true that many of the geometer's *a priori* laws, as well as his concepts, have been *suggested* by actual forms in nature. Knowledge starts in knowing concrete realities. But the thought, acting on these suggesting forms, creates ideal products and extends conclusions beyond the observed phenomena, and reaches necessary and universal principles of being. The whole system of geometrical truth, as well as of arithmetical, is, therefore, a creation of thought under the laws of subjective mental action.

Now the impressively significant thing is that these truths which thus come out of the mind, when applied to nature are found to tally with the realities in the actual structure of the universe. Mind and matter, two realities known in sense-perception and consciousness as actually existing, if anything is known to exist, though possessing no common attributes, and incapable of being resolved into one and the same thing, are yet found perfectly adapted to each other in all the laws which respectively regulate them in their independent action. The laws that appear in the one answer to the laws that hold in the other. This fact is illustrated on every hand:

It appears in the *law of equivalents and multiple proportions, under which all chemical combinations* are found to occur. The uniting atomic weights conform to a mathematically ascertained order. What the laws of thought require for true numerical ratios or proportions is discovered to be the actual rule under which nature works in her great chemical laboratory. The subjective movements of mind and the objective movements of physical substances recognize common standards.

It is seen in *crystallization*. "Crystals, we are told, may be studied from two points of view; first, as products of pure thought, like the solids of geometry; and, secondly, as objects of natural history; and the specimens found in nature, as far as examined, are discovered to correspond to the deductions of geometry." In the relations of their sides and angles, they are expressible in the formulæ of mathematical proportions. Crystallization is found to take place according to the laws of orderly thought.

The *laws of sound* are reducible to mathematical statement. The harmonies of music are well known to arise from certain fixed ratios in the vibrations of sonorous bodies. These ratios correspond to the orderly relations called for in arithmetical thought. The laws of the mind's knowing and of the world's constitution answer to each other in this.

Vegetable growth conforms to this principle of numerical symmetry. The leaves of plants are always arranged in spirals about the stem; and both the number of leaves and the number of turns of the spiral are always the same for any given plant. A comparison of different plants shows that these numbers, whatever they may be, stand in the relation of an orderly proportion. The simplest arrangement is that in which there are two leaves for each turn of the spiral; another arrangement completes the turn with three; still another completes two turns with five leaves. Taking various plants and writing out the relations between the number of leaves and turns of the spiral, we obtain, in succession, the fractions a regularly ascending series in which any two combined will make the next, while the numerator of any one added to the denominator of the preceding gives the denominator of the fraction whose numerator is employed. These numerical relations are found holding in the scales of every cone and bud, in the order of the bracts about the blossoms of the daisy, and in the position of every leaf on every plant. They do not belong only to the present flora of our globe. They are found in fossil botany. Plants have been constructed on the same general plan from the beginning. The same mathematical spiral which regulates the formation of a pine cone in one of our own woods governed their formation in the earliest geological forests which we dig up from beneath hundreds of feet of solid rock.

When we pass out into the distant regions of *astronomy*, we find the most impressive examples of the fact we are illustrating. In the solar system, the intervals between the planets, with the exception of Neptune, go on doubling, or nearly so, as we recede from the sun. And when we compare the *periodic times* of their revolutions, beginning with the most distant, we discover that we have for Uranus about one-half that of Neptune, for Saturn one-third that of Uranus, for Jupiter two-fifths that of Saturn, for the asteroids three-eighths that of Jupiter, for Mars about five-thirteenths that of the asteroids, for Venus eight-twenty-firsts that of Mars, and for Mercury about thirteen-thirty-fourths of that of Venus. The time of the earth is slightly exceptional. Writing out the numbers of this order,

and comparing them with those in vegetation, it is seen that we have the same series of fractions in the arrangement of leaves on plants and in the periods of the heavenly bodies. The mental order that fixes mathematical formulæ serves to express the facts not only in nature immediately around us, but in the movements of far-off worlds. There is thus seen to be an exact adaptation of the laws of mind to the realities of the objective constitution of the universe. The sciences are all crystallizing in mathematical form. We can take these creations of pure thought from human mind, and measure the actual distances and motions in the far-away heavens, determine the planetary orbits, future conjunctions of starry worlds, and eclipses that will be visible in centuries to come. The mind's products are adjusted by *its* laws into the same mould as the realities of the universe are by *their* laws. This is not only a fact of amazing adaptation of the independent action of the mind to the realities of the cosmic system, but one that clearly points to the intellectual Cause of the universe. It exhibits thought answering to thought. The universe is constructed according to mental laws. The *a priori* truths, intuitively appearing as necessary in mathematical relations in time and space, are found to have been actualized in the universe from the beginning. "Plato's conic sections and Euclid's division into extreme and mean ratio were made and used long before the days of Plato or Euclid, in the forms of earth and the orbits of the heavenly bodies."

Here we must close these illustrations of final cause in nature. They might be continued to any extent, for nature is jewelled with them everywhere. Acting for ends is an omnipresent feature in the constitution and movement of the world. Nature is conceded to be a great system, in well-adjusted and consistent unity; and when final cause is found to be the determining cause in one part, it means that this principle pervades it everywhere, and gives the universal order and consistency. These examples, therefore, are sufficient—typical of nature's whole method. They leave no room whatever to doubt the point which it has been the sole object of this section to establish, that nature does exhibit facts of finality, facts so clear, constant, and pervading as to prove finality to be an unquestionable principle of its action.

SECTION III

FINAL CAUSE IN NATURE DEMANDS INTELLIGENCE AND WILL

The point to be shown in this section is that these adjusted adaptations in nature must be referred to an intelligent predetermining Will. Finality has its necessary correlate in *intentionality*. This identifies the cause as a Personal Being.

In the face of the spontaneous conclusion men draw from adaptation to a designer, it may seem almost superfluous to go through the labor of presenting reasons to sustain this further and concluding point in the teleological syllogism. That "design," in the sense of a structured adaptation of means to an end, implies a designer, seems so nearly a self-evident proposition, that we are at first at a loss to understand how there can be any room for doubt, or for proof to remove doubt. But, as already mentioned, a real distinction is asserted, and objectors claim that the proof of adaptations in nature is still short of the proof of an intelligent author. For instance, Hume says, in substance: "The argument from design is simply analogical. But we have no right to assume that because we know from experience that houses, ships, watches, or other arrangements which we produce in the order of the world about us are due to this cause, therefore this is the only cause that can produce orderly arrangement. For aught we know, there may be other causes besides mind for orderly arrangement—that to make the kind of causation we find in ourselves the necessary cause for the order of the whole system of things is to make man the measure of the universe." J. S. Mill repeats the objection, and calls the conclusion which assumes mind as the only possible cause of acting for ends "an outrageous stretch of inference." The amount of the objection in this form, it will be observed, offers no positive disproof of the dependence of finality on an intelligent cause, but only suggests that there *may* be some other cause for it, only raises a faint or possible doubt, and then claims that the theistic conclusion falls short of a full demonstration. This claim is helped into plausibility by pantheistic or semi-pantheistic philosophies. The soul of nature is represented as itself the principle of all things, working not as a transcendent God, but as an internal or immanent blind principle. This is the substance of explanation by Hegel's "idea," and by Schopenhauer's unconscious "will." The theories emphasize all the facts of contrast between nature and art. They point out, especially, that the finality which works in man's industry is external to its product. But in nature it is internal, working as an inward force. Instinct is given as the completest type of the process. It is illustrated also in the production of organisms. In these the movement is inherent and self-contained. In this difference it is claimed that the true analogy between human industry and nature's products is broken. Human mechanism produces nothing that shows this peculiar immanent force; nature's works are characterized by this, and thus show the possible action of a principle other than mental intentionality, which in itself must suffice for all that it does. The "end" is not sought or found by any intelligent or conscious apprehension and pursuit, but appears out of the eternal conformity of things to their simple essence. "In nature the cause attains its end by self-development."

Leading materialists have been endeavoring to reinforce this denial of an intelligent cause for finality by claiming that the modern hypothesis of evolution suggests how conformity to the end in organisms can originate without any intermingling of an intelligence, by the blind administration of a law of nature. A fortuitous development in atomic and molecular structure, under a law of survival of forms best fulfilling conditions of stability, it is asserted, is sufficient, in its action from an infinitely remote past, to have fixed those formations which now look like intended adaptations in the midst of the whole evolution. It is all credited as a mere result of laws inherent in the blind movement. The only finality, it is said, is the finality of the forces immanent or inherent in matter itself. Hæckel says: "The history of evolution convinces us that the highly purposive and admirably constituted sense-organs, like all other organs, have developed without premeditated aim." It is needful, therefore, to consider this point and complete the teleological argument by presenting some of the evidence on which we are justified in taking the actual finality found to pervade nature as the proper and sufficient proof of a supreme *intelligent* First Cause.

1. The first thing to be considered is that *intelligence is at once the natural explanation of adaptation of means to ends, and the* ONLY *cause of which we know*. We know mind, as an intelligent, voluntary agent, to be the cause of design continually. We know this by consciousness. If we do not know this, we know nothing; our knowledge is actual zero. By observation and the communications of our fellow-men, we know them to be the authors of arrangement and contrivance. Personality, or intelligent will, has filled all lands and all centuries with purposive activities and structured works. The characterizing feature of the products of human industry is that they reveal a designer at every point, and establish the law of finality as a law of mind. They identify adaptation to ends as a *mental* function. If we wish to know the source of objective design, *i.e.*, of planned structures, we always find it, through the entire range of the world's activity in all times and climes, in a designing intelligence, and in this alone. Even on the mere ground of induction, therefore, there would be, to say the least, as much force and validity in this proof as for any scientific conclusion whatever. For the induction is complete and universal, unembarrassed by a single contrary fact for a counter induction. The unbroken experience and knowledge of the race have found adaptive industries explained only in intelligence. We know mind to be a cause that acts for ends through adaptation of select means, and we know of no other cause. Consciousness reveals no other. Science, working down among elements and molecules, and up to suns and stellar systems, detects no other. The supposed possibility of any other is sustained by no evidence

whatever. The suggestion has nothing to back it. Mind, therefore, has been left to us as the only known cause or explanation of specialized adaptation and structure. It is surely scientific to follow where the whole induction points. It is absurdly irrational to reject this in favor of some utterly unknown but supposed possibility.

So directly does this become the rational and necessary interpretation of finality, that opponents of the argument are compelled to concede its weight. For instance, J. S. Mill, though he has represented it as involving "an outrageous stretch of inference," feels forced to admit that design has not been eliminated from nature, or the necessity of referring it to intelligence overcome. In his *Essays on Religion,* he says: "The particular combination of organic elements called the eye had, in every instance, a beginning in time, and must, therefore, have been brought together by a cause, or causes. The number of instances is immeasurably greater than is, by the principles of the inductive logic, required for the exclusion of a random concurrence of independent causes, or, speaking technically, for the elimination of chance. We are, therefore, warranted by the canons of induction in concluding that what brought all these elements together was some cause common to them all; and inasmuch as the elements agree in the single circumstance of conspiring to produce sight, there must be some connection by way of causation between the cause which brought these elements together and the fact of sight…. The natural sequel to the argument would be this: Sight, being a fact not precedent but subsequent to the putting together of the organic structure of the eye, can only be connected with the production of that structure in the character of a final, not an efficient cause. But this at once marks the origin as proceeding from an intelligent Will."

The force of this evidence is increased by the discriminating *recognition* which mind has for its own peculiar working and products. It includes not simply the fact that we know intelligence to be a cause of specialized adaptations, and we know of no other, but still more, that in those processes of finality found in nature the human mind directly and positively recognizes the intelligence it is compelled to postulate.

Spontaneously mind knows its own everywhere, discriminating it by direct insight from every other kind of working. In knowing itself it has fellowship with universal mind. When it meets mind, wherever acting, it recognizes it. We thus not only know it to be a cause of adaptation of means to purposed ends, beyond which we know of no other, but we identify its presence by a kind of intuitive necessity. We do not simply *infer* that intelligence must be working here, but we *find* it here. Nature, in so many of its laws and products, is so truly the concrete language of adjustive thought, it is so clearly the engraved page of a designed expression, the embodiment of a rational idea, that the human mind reads intelligence there as it reads it on a printed page. It is in no unknown tongue, but in the language of universal mind. The wisdom and working shining out from nature attest themselves as the working and wisdom of a Thinker. In the very adaptation which the mind finds in itself to the study and interpretation of nature, it becomes aware that the world is a thought, an actual expression of an orderly and intelligent plan. There is, therefore, one cause and only one known to the human mind for finality, and by spontaneous rational insight that is recognized and identified as the actual cause. For it is just the signs of intelligence that the mind finds. To deny the force of this is equivalent to asserting that unconsciousness may act the part of intelligence, or contradictories may work as the same.

We have thus, even in this first point, the natural and legitimate conclusion from the data—a conclusion warranted as an induction from universal experience. No scientific truth whatever rests on an induction so complete and impressive. It is not, indeed, a "demonstration," for the subject does not admit of that kind of proof; but it is the kind of evidence on which all the practical interests of life are necessarily directed. This conclusion as to the connection between intelligence and the pursuit of special ends is the universal conviction of the unsophisticated judgment of the race. And it is the conclusion, too, when the most careful scrutiny is made into the facts, and these facts are interpreted by the best principles of the inductive logic. It cannot, therefore, be justly set aside until objectors shall have shown some other explanation better sustained.

2. The *immanence* of finality in nature, offered as obviating the necessity of a creative intelligence, entirely fails to answer the purpose for which it is alleged. The fact that the forces work internally in nature is not disputed. We fully admit that its finality, whether in organic processes or in instincts, is accomplished through principles which work from within. The point of their proximate action is not from without. This is one of the acknowledged differences between the finality of nature and that of human mechanism. The energy, whatever it may be, works within the processes, and not as an artificer standing outside. In this respect growth is different from the work of man's industry. The blind inner force tends to an end, as if self-moving. The actual process goes on by an interior principle—a principle locally contained in nature itself. But the insufficiency of this fact, when offered as a solution supposed to nullify the need of a designing mind, becomes clear in recalling three points:

(1) Internal or immanent finality does not necessarily mean a *simply immanent cause*. That is, it does not necessarily exclude a cause starting back of the blind force that is internally working to its end. Examples illustrating the reality of the agency of mind behind processes that work internally and blindly are about us every day. The chronometer, acting in interior adaptation for marking time as if it meant to do so, is not explained in its own immanent force and action. The finality has been lodged for a time in the intrinsic structure. Though the forces work interiorly, they do not exclude an intentional and transcendent cause. Or, take an illustration clearly within the sphere of nature. We constantly observe in men action moving blindly or instinctively to useful ends, lodged as hereditary mental and dispositional traits which have been incorporated primarily by intentional activity. A similar result appears in the modified action of instinct, and even of organization itself, under the training, by man, of the domesticated animals. The organisms and instincts of nature exhibit no finality that is absolute or underived, and that may not have an intelligent cause. Take an individual organism. The individual is not the cause of itself. Or a species—a species is not its own cause. The forces which work immanently in both individuals and species are not *absolutely* or restrictively

immanent. The immanence found is only *relative,* and thus does not exclude an intentional cause. If it be said that "a seed virtually contains all the constituent parts of the plant produced from it, and that its development is only directed toward its preservation," it is in point to reply that this finality in the seed, not being absolute, may itself, with all the laws which have produced it, be due to a primary purposive cause.

(2) This immanent force, supposed to be blindly acting as a final cause, not being primitive or absolute, but derived and relative, not only *allows* an intelligent purpose as the real cause behind it, but *requires it, unless unknown causation is preferred to known.* For, to take the best form of such internal finality, *instinct,* this, not being the cause of itself, is not the full true cause of its products. It is not a cause in the real sense at all, but only a *carrier* of forces and laws through a fixed movement to its product. To offer this as the full account of it is the absurdity of pointing to a part of a process as showing the determining cause of it all. For the specialized ends, therefore, to which instinct always works, but of which it knows nothing, we are obliged to find a cause in a conscious intelligence that has organized the instinct. An unconscious intelligence is a contradiction in terms, as truly as would be "round squares." Instinct itself is a specialized adaptation to all that comes out of it, and needs itself to be accounted for. Its property is that it precisely resembles a work calculated and arranged beforehand. And for the predetermination that acts in it and through it, intelligence is the natural and only rational explanation.

(3) The claim that inherent and underived forces of nature have produced the actual order and adaptations of the universe, without knowing either ends or means, resolves itself into the theory of mere blind evolution. It means that the energies of matter moved to the results which have been reached by their intrinsic laws in self-direction and self-limitation. This theory, strictly viewed, displaces final cause itself. Still, as it does not destroy or blot out the actual facts of order and adaptation from the world, it is necessary to take the claim into consideration. This claim, however, when examined in its last analysis, is simply to revert to the hypothesis of chance. It rests in absolute

materialism, and sees in matter the supposed "potency of all things." It views the atoms as eternal and having in themselves and their underived modes of motion and interaction the real and only power to which the order of the universe in both nature and man is to be credited. Scientific speculation shapes the theory variously; but whatever shape is given to it, it furnishes no other solution of the actual finality pervading nature than such as leaves it fundamentally the work of chance. The consideration of this must be our next point.

3. That this finality requires an intelligent author is impressively certain from the fact that *a denial of such cause throws us back on chance.* That this is the true and inevitable alternative to intentionality has already been shown. Chance is no denial of cause, but of design. It means mere *coincidence,* a fortuitous result of forces acting without purpose, but giving origin to products that prove useful, as imagined in that kind of motion and evolution which is said to form organisms and adapt them to their actual ends without any guiding design. Can the order, adaptation, harmony, and consistency of the constitution of things, all its manifest subjection to the law of utility and beauty, be rationally referred to chance? This is the question to be answered at this point. Every denial of intentionality for finality is an affirmation of the sufficiency of chance. For there is no other alternative. The *reductio ad absurdum,* therefore, applied to this affirmation, will be a proof of the authorship of nature in a creative intelligence.

Let us, for argument's sake, suppose matter to be eternal—a supposition, however, in open conflict with all its characteristics of finiteness and dependence. The starting point, then, for our world and the universe, as they have now come to be, must have been the potency of the atoms, whatever they may be. There is no cause back of them. See how the case stands. There are countless millions of millions of them. But the universe, as we find it, is manifestly one, a single, magnificent, complex, but harmonious system. Its most impressive characteristic is the unity in variety and the variety in unity, that mark it in all its parts and as a stupendous whole. The unity that appears in a single organ, say an eye, is not more unquestionable than that in which the solar system acts together, or starry systems unite with starry systems. How could these atoms, moving blindly, form the universe into such marvelous unity and order? There is not a particle of evidence that a dormant but germinal intelligence—the so-called "unconscious intelligence"—belongs essentially to the atoms. Even if it did belong to them, it would be unspeakably absurd to suppose that they could by unanimous counsel agree to work to a common plan. For, between such rudimentary or unborn intelligence and the counsel, thought, and forecast seen in nature's finality, the disproportion is infinite. Nothing short of omniscience itself could have sufficed for the work these atoms had on hand. But could they combine by mere chance, and by chance interaction produce such a universe as that in which we live, and of which we form a part? It is evident that there must be millions to one against these atoms, as they jostle age after age together, producing even the simplest structures or organisms that mark the course of nature—and millions to one that chance action of atoms would pull down and destroy any thus happening to occur.

But even were we to suppose, despite this tremendous improbability, that chance could produce and continue in existence some useful combinations, still the difficulty of thus accounting for all the elaborate and beneficent adaptations which everywhere illuminate nature would be multiplied a thousand fold at every step of the attempt. The chances against the more complex combinations, dependent on the simpler and more elementary, and against the stability of the higher, grow so clearly in geometrical progression, that it soon becomes a mathematical certainty that without a teleological plan the world must forever remain a chaos. Atheistic evolutionism has sorely felt this difficulty, and to save the case has been wont, with other expedients, to fall back on the supposed greatness of the time. "Accidental variations" of accidental combinations, becoming, somehow, stable through their usefulness, surviving because of their fitness with environment, have been spoken of as able, in the countless ages of the earth, to have transmuted the chaos into a cosmos. But unfortunately for the hypothesis, as has often been pointed out, time, whose help is supposed to suffice, is not a cause of anything, but only a multiplier, and when, as in this case, what we have to multiply is a principle of confusion, order cannot be the product. Time may afford scope and field for an intelligent, selecting, arranging, and unifying *mind* to produce an orderly system, of harmonized parts and for beneficent purpose, but affords no explanation whatever how chance movements of an infinity of blind or even potentially conscious atoms, could issue in a universe whose fundamental and most characteristic action no longer exhibits any sign of chance. For, in the genuine and best inductive science and philosophy of to-day the word "chance" has no place or recognition; it is a thought utterly irreconcilable with the reign of wise law and manifest order everywhere.

Further, to set forth more fully, if possible, the absurdity of crediting the fortuitous movements of matter, as in any atheistic hypothesis of either ancient or modern evolution, with the production of the present universe, so rich in wide-reaching and marvellous adaptations, we must put it under the light of the mathematical doctrine of chances. Take a particular organ—the eye. In this organ physiology points out at least thirteen distinct particulars, the failure of any one of which would result in failure of vision. Assuming the chance of each of these particulars being developed without design in embryonic life to be equal to the chance of its not being developed, and therefore represented by one-half—as of a penny's falling head or tail—then, since the probability of the concurrence of the thirteen conditions is obtained by multiplying into each other the fractions denoting the probability of each condition taken singly, the likelihood of the production of the eye by chance would be represented by That is, there would be 8,192 chances against one of its being so made. This, however, would denote only the improbability of such origin of a single eye. But eyes occur in pairs all through nature. For the conjunction of the two, in any one person, that improbability would be doubled. Against the repetition of the occurrence in the countless millions of eyes, the chances would be increased to inexpressible figures.

But this is only the beginning. For the production of any one particular in the eye, thousands of molecules must concur to the same end. How little probability of their doing so accidentally, will appear from some mathematical calculations of the various combinations possible in chance movements. The play of combinations possible out of ten different units, or the number of changes that may be rung on ten bells, is 3,628,800. The different combinations that may be made with the twenty-six letters of the alphabet require twenty-seven places of figures to express them. Prof. Jevons has calculated that in the game of whist, with a pack of fifty-two cards, four hands of thirteen being held simultaneously, the number of distinct deals becomes so vast as to require for its statement twenty-eight places of figures, and says that if the whole population of the world, say a hundred thousand millions of persons, were to deal cards day and night for a hundred millions of years they would not in that time have exhausted a hundred thousandth part of the possible deals. It seems in the highest degree improbable that one game of whist has ever been exactly like another, except by intention. In the light of such figures, expressing the almost infinite uncertainties of the play of random combinations, the improbability becomes evident, that the countless molecules should fortuitously combine to produce the finely ordered and adjusted parts of the eye, or that all the different and needful chemical elements should thus unite, in their proportionate quantities, to form each and all of the organs, and the union of organs, in the body.

To understand the nature of the problem it must be remembered that the molecules are combined not only in different numbers and proportions, but in successive accumulations, each union becoming a unit for a further and dependent union. The primary unions are only the beginning of nature's action. Unions are built on unions, in increasing complexity, system on system. The atoms combine in molecules, the molecules form cells, the cells build organs, the organs arrange themselves cooperatively into organisms or individuals, and the individuals form a dualism for the continuance of races. Each step in the order of dependent correlations passes into vaster ranges of the play of permutation. Take, in illustration, the unities which may be made with the twenty-six letters of our alphabet. With these may be formed several trillions of words.

With these words may be constructed an immensely larger number of sentences. With these sentences a still greater number of books can be made. With these books still a higher diversity of libraries. This last is what mathematicians call a combination of the "fifth order." An example of this is given in the arrangement of two units in all possible ways in ascending rank: First step, 2; next step, 4; third step, 16; fourth step, 65,536; fifth step, 65,536 twos multiplied together, making a number so great as to require 19,729 places of figures. "The problem," it has well been said, "involved in undisguised atheism is to derive the uniformities by which we live and move and have our being, from generation to generation, from chance combinations when increased to infinite orders of the powers of infinity." These figures make it as certain as applied mathematics can make anything that the material elements could not have given the world its intelligible method and filled it with its wonders of orderly subservience to utility and pleasure, by any merely inherent, blind, and undesigning cause. To believe that the poems of Homer and Milton or the histories of Motley and Bancroft might be but accidental products of the blind interaction of the letters of the alphabet, would not surpass the credulity of crediting to chance the poems and history of nature's universal movement.

The force of this cannot be set aside by saying, as has often been said, that the almost infinitely probable may yet occur—that while there may be trillions on trillions against one, yet the one may happen, when infinite time allows all possible combinations. This could avail only if the possible combinations could be conceived of as running on in regular order without reversion through the possible series. But such orderly progress through these combinations, so as to try all and preserve the useful, is itself a manifest subordination to plan and a contradiction to chance. It is clear that the movement might otherwise pass very often through similar combinations, or replace its own attained order with confusion, and so, despite the infinite time, fail to exhaust the false conditions for the true.

Nor is the force of this evidence evaded by adopting the statement which is wont to affirm these adaptations to ends as simply "the necessary conditions of existence." It is alleged that the forces of nature have taken the course they have in virtue of their own inherent and eternal laws, in the blindest chance, indeed, but deflected out of chaos and continued in better and better adaptive movement just because these combinations have in them the conditions of coherence and stability. The molds of the non-adjusted are broken and disappear. The orderly remain because they are stronger. "The survival of the fittest" expresses the weakness of disorder in comparison with order, the strength and permanence which the serviceable gets from its own serviceableness in the struggle of existence.

But this expression, "conditions of existence," is ambiguous, and when cleared of its obscurities, fails to be an explanation. It may mean either of two things. (1) It may be taken in its absolute sense, that only what is orderly and coordinated to use can exist. In this sense, the assertion is utterly without foundation. For a chaos has as much chance to exist as a cosmos, and by the very theory of chance the cosmos only comes in by the slightest possibility. Unorganized and amorphous masses actually exist, and have their "conditions of existence," much easier than useful organizations. The latter have comparatively poor chance in the struggle of being. Simply to find "conditions of existence "nature need not ascend to the higher forms at all. (2) It may be taken in a relative sense—that an organism can be what it is, and fulfil its functions, only on condition that its parts are adjusted as they are. Then it is no explanation whatever of its *origin,* and furnishes no reason why it should hold its place at all against the powers of inorganic nature which in fact crumble every individual one into dust. The strings and its other adjusted parts are the "necessary conditions" of a harp, but this is by no means a showing that the harp exists without the agency of an intelligent maker. Apart from this, what necessity is there for the existence of the harp at all? It is just from its fulfilling the conditions of being a harp that we know it has been made by intelligence and not by chance. The adaptation of the parts of an organism of nature, both to each other and to their environment, is indeed the necessary condition of the existence and relative stability of such organism in its specific and distinguishing character, but it is just this complete adaptation, with such stability of it, that chance is unable to furnish a reason for. The true state of the matter is this: The field of existence being so much vaster and easier in the lower range of unorganized combinations, the alleged "conditions," when sifted, are not "necessary "conditions of *existence* at all, but conditions of something far higher and rational, *i.e.,* of happiness, utility, subservience to the ideals and needs of a rational system up into which they reach. The truth is that it is just this finality found *beyond* the grade which may be sunk from view in the mere essentials of existence, that pushes forward the great problem whose solution we are seeking, but for whose rational explanation no causal forces short of that of prearranging intelligence are found satisfactorily competent. Such intelligence we know unquestionably to be the appropriate and specific cause of finality. Atheism, in rejecting this cause, is compelled to have recourse to some form of the hypothesis of chance.

4. *The leading explanations of the hypothesis of evolution concede the necessity of a creative ordaining intelligence for all that nature includes from its start.* It is this hypothesis that has given plausibility to the supposed competency of the immanent and fortuitous causality already noticed. It is proper to consider, more distinctly, the bearings on theism of this view of nature, accepted now in greater or less degree by many leading scientists. It asserts no cause of finality except such as is found in mind.

The hypothesis of evolution may be viewed as including more or less. (1) As including less: There is unquestionably some firmly established scientific truth expressed by this term. The world of to-day, so full of order and adaptations, was not made as it is, at once. It was not produced by a single act of power, in the form, aspect, and completeness we now see, crowded and adorned with the life and structures which now appear. Geology leaves no room to doubt that our very rocks, hills, and mountains have appeared under changes in which the earth has advanced from conditions in which what now is was not. Paleontology leaves no doubt that both vegetable and animal life in the early geological ages was simpler and of lower order than that which fills the earth now. The things that are made have come to be as they are through a development or progressive movement out of a very remote past and by a process in some respects gradual. Beyond all doubt there has been *some* kind of evolution for the history of the earth, and we must put the creative design and word to work far back in the depth of the ages. (2) As including more: An evolution, favored by scientists of great name as a "working hypothesis," which teaches as probable that all forms of both vegetable and animal life have been naturally evolved, from primordial germs, say in the forms of protoplasm, and have been gradually differentiated and improved by accumulated and accumulating characteristics, through natural descent, into the earth's present flora and fauna, man included. In this view the doctrine of direct creation is superseded by that of an evolution by slow and gradual advance and ascent through countless ages, until at last the present orders of plants, races of animals and man appear as the lineal descendants of the earliest and lowest organizations. Darwinism has been the leading phase of this hypothesis, as being the most elaborate attempt to explain on this theory of descent, not only the origin and structure of the irrational animals, but of man himself, under the action of "natural selection and survival of the fittest." Of such descent from preexisting species, various subordinate hypotheses present differing explanations. Some picture the transition as sudden and divinely planned. Others as made naturally by changes too gradual to be perceived except in widely separated stages.

Of this evolutionary teaching, in this full sense, it is to be noted:

(1) It is only a hypothesis. Though believed by many, it has not been proved. It is not to be looked upon as demonstrated or even scientifically established truth, but as a provisional "working hypothesis," to be allowed only so much weight as the facts and reasons given entitle it. But even were it scientifically established, it would not remove the difficulty of atheism, or destroy the proofs of theism.

(2) The theory does not obliterate from nature the actual *facts* of finality. These are still around and in us, unchanged by the theory, clear and impressive. If evolution and finality should indeed be irreconcilable, then the omnipresent order of nature would be evermore discrediting the theory. These perpetual,

strong, clear, ineradicable facts teach finality more impressively than any other facts can teach evolution.

(3) But evolution in its very nature is not a *cause*, but only a *mode*. It gives only the *order of the process* through which the cause has been operating. It seeks to set forth the method by which the cause, whatever it be, has worked. In no just sense, therefore, can it be held as necessarily excluding design. Prof. Huxley is right when he admits that in this view of the world, the teleologist always has the advantage of being able to defy his opponent to show that the present arrangements were not from the very first *intended* to be brought about. The effect of evolution, therefore, were it regarded as established in the full form which teaches the derivative origin of species, would simply be, in this connection, to throw back the point from which the designing cause has been actually working to a remoter past. Evolution could evolve only what was *in*volved in the forces and laws at the very beginning. The effect, then, would be to make the design sweep through longer range and wider field. The plan revealed in the issue may be viewed as provided for in the very atoms and their given laws. Our discovery of laws is no contradiction of ends.

It is true, materialists have used this hypothesis as an occasion for rejecting all teleology. Denying all substantive existence except matter in the universe, they have claimed it as obviating all necessity of assuming a predetermining intelligence for the production of the world, and as showing how atomic and molecular mechanics, in their intrinsic laws, may have formed things as they are. But as their explanation, necessarily and according to their own confession, falls back upon either immanent finality or chance, or both, no further answer is needed than that already given under those heads.

(4) Evolutionists of highest rank themselves claim that the evidences from design for an intelligent Creator are not overthrown or weakened by the hypothesis.

A. R. Wallace, who was an independent co-originator of the "selection theory," says: "Why should we suppose the machine too complicated to have been designed by the Creator so complete that it would necessarily work out harmonious results?

Richard Owen, one of England's most eminent scientists, says: "Natural evolution, through secondary causes, by means of slow physical and organic operations through long ages, is not the less clearly recognizable as the act of an all-adaptive Mind, because we have abandoned the old error of supposing it the result of a primary, direct, and sudden act of creational construction."

Prof. Huxley admits: "There is a wider teleology which is not touched by the doctrine of evolution, but is actually based on the fundamental proposition of evolution."

St. George Mivart: "Even 'design' and 'purpose' are recognized as quite compatible with evolution."

Prof. Asa Gray, one of the most decided evolutionists of our land, says: "What is lost in directness may perhaps be gained in breadth and depth.... The natural history of ends becomes consistent and reasonably intelligible under the light of evolution. As the forms and kinds rise gradually out of that which was well nigh formless into consummate form, so do biological ends rise and assert themselves in increasing distinctness and variety. Vegetables and animals have paved the earth with intentions."

Even Prof. John Fiske, whose enthusiastic Darwinism has led him into most daring speculations, affirms: "The doctrine of evolution does not allow us to take the atheistic view of man.... He who recognizes the slow and subtle process of evolution as the way in which God makes things come to pass, must take a far higher view.... The Darwinian theory, properly understood, replaces as much teleology as it destroys. From the first dawning of life we see all things working together toward one mighty goal, the evolution of the most exalted spiritual qualities which characterize humanity."

As to the amount of truth that may underlie the hypothesis of evolution, or its value as a scientific speculation, this discussion is not directly concerned. Formidable difficulties are in the way of its successfully explaining many of the phenomena of nature. The winnowing away of its chaff and the saving of whatever wheat may be in it may be safely left to Christian science and thought. It is enough for our purpose, in this connection, to note that according to the claims of its representative advocates, the theory is not necessarily non-teleological, and cannot be worked without assuming a coordinating intelligence. In whatever conflict it may stand with other aspects of Christian truth, it furnishes no disproof of the theistic evidences from design.

5. But the crowning evidence that the finality of nature is due to an intelligent cause is found in the *existence of human mind* and its *supremacy* in the world. Intelligent, self-determining personality is the highest fact in the actual world. We must have a sufficient reason for its existence, and for all that it contains. Apart from an infinite intelligence as creator of mind, the existence of human personality and its power over nature are an insoluble mystery. We are aware, indeed, of the materialist's theory of deriving human mind from material organization, as a product and manifestation of molecular action. But besides the fact that this explanation has commanded the assent of but a very small number of thinkers, and is contradicted by incontrovertible data of psychology, there are considerations which show that even were it accepted it would fail to annul the necessity of a creative intelligence. For the creative energy that shows itself intelligent in the end must be held as intelligent in the beginning—unless the cause can give to the effect more than lies in its own powers. A number of points are to be looked at:

(1) Mind actually exists. Even those who speak of it as a product of brain action admit that it *is*. There is such a thing as intelligent will, self-directing personality, in the world. It is a power.

(2) The materialist's theory, which holds the human mind as a product of brain organization, will not work without an adaptive intelligence back of the organization. If mind results from the molecular action to which the hypothesis credits it, then that action must be adapted to produce it. And the adaptation thus involved could be considered as no slight or inferior grade of adaptation, but the most elaborate and exact, the subtlest and finest of which we can conceive. It is an adaptation the farthest possible from chance. If the brain be not only the organ of mind, but the producer of mind, with all its laws of order, a very cosmos within the cosmos, the summit of nature where its whole action

becomes purposive and reveals a justifying reason for all inferior movement, then the brain itself must not only be the most startling fact of finality, but a peculiar evidence of designed construction. On this theory, the two terms, the cause and the effect, the molecular action and the mental product, are here in immediate connection; and if the molecular action furnishes intelligence, like a rising light suddenly illuminating all the scene, it is difficult to believe that no spark of intelligence was concerned in providing the molecular action. Out of matter, into mind—the bloom of nature into free intelligence is too interpretative to be regarded as brought about, and so wisely maintained, by blind atomics alone.

The wonder of all wonders would be, if a system of nature with no mind behind it, with no predetermined order lodged within it, with no arranged end for its processes, all moving by chance and blind force, should suddenly, at this precise point in man's mental life, emerge into a realm of intelligence, will, and purposive activity. At the close of a long series of powers moving only in blind, necessitated action, the series is at once changed into self-conscious intellect, self-directing will, a world of free personality, ruled by mental laws. Upon what law of merely physical succession and continuity could such a phenomenon be explained? To suppose no intelligence for this adaptation of brain for the intelligence that appears in its product, is not to assert, as materialists pretend, a scientific law of cause and effect in the appearance of mind, but to abandon the law of causation, to assert an event without adequate cause. For then this asserted function of the brain for thought would be credited to chance, and chance would have to be installed maker, both of the realm of nature and the realm of all the high, free, purposive action of mankind. Even on the materialist's hypothesis, therefore, the existence of self-directing human intelligence demands, with inexorable logic, the existence of an intelligent Creator.

(3) But the conclusion thus required, even on the basis of materialism, becomes stronger when the human mind is correctly viewed as something other and higher than a mere manifestation of matter. As mentioned in a preceding chapter, science has been unable to show any explanation of the origin of mind in any or all

of the physical forces. Across the transitions between dead matter and sensation, sensation and consciousness, consciousness and intelligent free will, no bridge of simply physical causation has ever been made perceptible. Even the mystery of "life" refuses the solution of the scalpel and retort; much more, if possible, does "mind" elude all explanation by the chemistries or known motions of matter. "That it cannot possibly be," says Prof. Fiske, "the product of any cunning arrangement of material particles is demonstrated beyond peradventure by what we know of the correlation of physical forces." Mind exists as a spiritual entity, with non-material attributes. It is the grand, crowning phenomenon of the earth. The very law of its existence is to act as a final cause. Thus it becomes the ruling reality in the world, down before which everything else bows and does homage. As an intelligent agent human mind penetrates the secrets of nature, reads the laws of its structures and movements, and generalizes its principles and facts into grand scientific systems. It discerns the vast harmonious adaptations throughout the world and far-off starry spheres, and in a wonder-working will, seizing hold of the forces and laws in the physical constitution of things, makes them servants to its wishes and welfare. But being itself a limited, dependent existence, it must have had an origin. For this origin there must be an adequate cause. Is the intelligence which thus turns and masters nature a mere passive and fortuitous product of the blind physical forces which it then analyzes and uses? Is this mind, so full of intentional activity that this kind of energy expresses the characteristic and law of its constitution, to be credited to a fortuitous origination and perpetuation by unconscious matter? Is this victory of finality to be counted as the triumph of a cause that never had a purpose? How should chance action establish the law of action with design?

(4) Stress must be laid upon this *freedom* of human personality. If man is in any real sense free, he cannot be the mere product of molecular action. If he is the pure creature of material motion, his actions must be as truly necessitated as the flow of the tides, the fall of rains, or the change of seasons, and his counsels and deeds, his aims and triumphs, are nothing but the ever on-going interaction of the molecules which compose

him. But the consciousness of the whole race testifies against the suggestion of any such law of necessity in human personality. It affirms an indubitable freedom; and this at once lifts mind into a sphere beyond the reach of physical causation. Can causes which act only in necessity create and endow a creature with the law of liberty and choice? The science which would interpret the cause of the human mind must take full account of all that it presents. It presents a wonderful complex of powers, with attributes irreducible to identity with those belonging to matter. It acts not only in self-determination, but in subjugating nature's plasticity and movements to its service. It has a history, written in ages of thought, skill, enterprise, institutions, moral systems, religions, arts, sciences, literature, philosophy. The pretense of accounting for man's personality, with all that it thus embraces and that reveals the nature of its essence, by the simple terms of material motion and force, can be plausible only if the contents of the problem are forgotten. It can have a seeming success only by dropping out of view the very attributes which characterize the phenomenon, the adequate cause of which we are seeking. There is a direct and adequate explanation in the creative energy of a supreme intelligent First Cause. But to resolve this whole world of human intelligence, with all its ages of activity and achievement, into dark, unconscious, impersonal causation of blind atoms, is in fact to abandon the law of causation. For the law requires *adequate* cause; but here there is an almost infinite disproportion between alleged cause and the actual effects.

6. It adds great weight to this conclusion, to remember that while these reasons call for an intelligent cause for the design found in nature, *the whole body of the inductive sciences rests upon this assumption.* The theistic conclusion is seen to be in harmony, not only with man's rational freedom and moral and religious constitution, but equally so with all the fundamental scientific necessities and interests. For science assumes that nature is really an orderly system, conformed to modes comprehensible by the thinking mind. It treats nature in its objective facts as answering to the interpretative order of the subjective reason. The very idea of "cause" answers in the mind's estimate of value as an explaining "reason." The universe is treated as a "thought,"

explicable under human scientific thought. Kepler's words: "O, God, I think Thy thoughts after Thee," expresses the real assumption which underlies rational science, even when it professedly repudiates the assumption. For it always seeks an expression of nature in the molds of mental order. It traces the relation of part to part and of part to the whole, and attempts to get at their *meanings* by a discovery of their rational relations to discoverable ends. It assumes teleology, and that a teleology in harmony with mental laws. The force of this is well summed up in the sentences with which President Porter concludes his *Intellectual Science:* "We analyze the several processes of knowledge into their underlying assumptions, and we find that the one assumption which underlies them all is a self-existent Intelligence, who not only can be known by man, but who *must* be known by man in order that man may know anything besides. In analyzing our psychological processes, we develop and demonstrate an ultimate truth, and that is the truth which the unsophisticated intellect of child and man requires and accepts, that there is a self-existent personal Intelligence, on whom the universe depends for the being and the relations of which it consists. We are, therefore, not alone justified, we are compelled, to conclude our analysis of the human intellect with the assertion that its processes involve the assumption that there is an uncreated Thinker, whose thoughts can be interpreted by the created intellect which is made in His image."

CHAPTER V

THE MORAL EVIDENCE

THE moral evidence is drawn from the existence of conscience and the facts of the moral system of the world. It includes the reality of man's moral nature and all the indications of an intended conformity of the race to immutable principles of righteousness. This evidence might be regarded as a branch of the teleological, as it traces a conformity in the ethical constitution of man and the world to the high ends of character and blessedness. It exhibits the highest range of final cause, for the lofty ends for which the whole system of inferior nature exists. But it deserves specific attention, as a particular proof, completing and crowning all the other evidences.

The facts on which the reasoning here proceeds are very large and impressive, and when grouped so as to exhibit their true and necessary meaning, their testimony becomes unmistakable. It will be enough for us to look at this evidence in the three chief forms into which it naturally falls.

1. *Directly from the existence and action of conscience in man.* Concerning this the following points must be noted:

(1) Whatever name may be given to this power, whether called "conscience" or the "moral sense," or the "moral faculty," or viewed as a complex of different powers, its existence as an integral part of the human constitution is unquestionable. It is a part of man's personality. In various degrees of development it is universal. In all ages and all tribes it has shown itself in asserting the distinction between right and wrong, affirming obligation to

do the one and avoid the other, and declaring the reality of duty and responsibility. In proportion as man is elevated, and the faculties which belong essentially to his nature are developed, this faculty—if it is to be so called—becomes clearer in its discernments, and stronger in its imperatives. Its existence is witnessed to in the earliest literatures of the race, in the language of every nation, in all law with its penalties, and all love with its rewards. In the highest culture into which the best progress has brought humanity, and in the latest analyses which science has attempted of the human constitution, conscience remains, not as a diminished, but a more prominent and impressive fact. The very latest speculations, instead of denying its existence, have felt obliged to offer explanations of it. Evolution wrestles with the fact, and offers its "data of ethics." Even materialism talks of morality, while denying its essential basis of free-will or self-determining personality. In some measure every man finds in his own mind a necessary and ineradicable distinction between right and wrong, and a conviction of an "*ought*" and "*ought not*" for himself and others. As a rational being, with faculties of knowledge, sensibility, and choice, he knows himself to be a moral agent, amenable to laws of right, out from under which there is no escape. He cannot cease to hold himself or others responsible. This capacity for moral distinctions, with its high imperative to seek the right, is the final characteristic of human personality.

(2) Its authority does not depend on any particular view of the nature of conscience. It is true that some accounts of it tend to unsettle its value for the moral life and weaken its testimony to the existence of immutable moral law. But after all fair reductions are made, enough remains to constitute a most unquestionable ethical authority, somehow or other established in man's constitution. There is no good reason to doubt the substantial correctness of the view which holds the distinction of right and wrong as a necessary idea of reason, and which looks on conscience as the reason's necessary perception of the moral quality of the actions of free agents, as conformed or not to the relations and perceived ends of being. It is, undoubtedly, fundamentally intellectual, and its action consists in directly

perceiving, in clearer or more imperfect way and according to the light enjoyed, this quality of right or wrong and the consequent obligation. Its function is not creative, but perceptive, of the moral relation it discerns, and of the duty which arises in and from it. The moral emotions, according to the psychological law under which the mental sensibilities are awakened only by knowing, follow and blend with this perception of moral quality and the obligation it involves. This view is adequately supported by the best established facts of psychology.

But even on a lower view of conscience—that, for instance, which represents the moral judgments as the product of circumstances and training, or that which, in the teaching of materialistic evolution, interprets them as "the results of accumulated experiences of utility, gradually organized and inherited"—the fact of a sense of moral obligation and responsibility remains. The fact, with all its well-known elements, is independent of any theory of explanation. Conscience does not cease to judge, or to hold men responsible to its discriminations, because men speculate about its origin or progressive development. It does not withdraw or tone down its claims, when the air is full of voices trying to show that it should not be so imperative. Unless man ceases to be man and falls out of his intrinsic personality, he must, day by day, confront the reality of moral distinctions, asserting themselves by an inexorable necessity of his reason, and holding him to them as supreme law for his life. And it is exceedingly interesting to notice that the latest view, as formulated by materialistic evolutionism, so far from teaching the downfall and disappearance of ethical law from man's nature, forecasts a future development of it continually toward the ideal standard of absolute or perfect morality. Even on these lower theories, therefore, the essential phenomena of conscience remain as facts to be accounted for. And whatever hypothesis may be framed in explanation of its genesis and development, it shows at least a most wonderful adaptation to the endowment and highest exaltation of man. If, indeed, a process of evolution by molecular mechanics and organic differentiation has not only developed from a chaos of atoms a world of intelligence and rational order, but enthroned a law of righteousness for the welfare of the race, it becomes the supreme exhibition of the teleological principle and its sovereignty for the whole system of things.

We are not required, however, nor even permitted, to interpret the conscience after any of these lower theories. Probably no more signal failures are anywhere to be found than the attempts to account for the realities in the moral perceptions by the accidental training of circumstances or in the experiences of utility and pleasure organized into permanent approval or rejection by a process of materialistic evolution. The idea of right is universally known to be generically distinct and different from that of utility, and nothing but confusion of thought can ever dream that they can be counted the same. To treat the distinction of right and wrong as the same as the distinction between utility and inutility, or between pleasure and discomfort, is not to account for moral distinctions, but to deny them. There is indeed a close relation between rightness and utility; but the real and logical order is, not that an action is right because it is useful, but it is useful because it is right. The conscience-perception discovers the right, irrespective of the question of utility or pleasure. In the distinction, therefore, between right and wrong, written ineffaceably in man's reason and irreducible to any other quality, there is found an enthroned law of obligation and responsibility. The reality of this law requires a moral lawgiver as the framer of his nature.

(3) The force of this is not annulled, but rather confirmed, by the diversity of the judgments of conscience, when the moral distinction comes to be applied to questions of duty in the relations of life.

For, *first*, the distinction is found to persist in the face of the greatest contrariety of judgment as to its particular applications. The law of imperative to the right may be real and inexorably authoritative, and yet in the practical relations of life men may find it difficult to determine the particular thing that is right. In regard to all the great fundamental ethical qualities, in their abstract conception, the conscience of the race has one voice round the globe and through all centuries. But as particular duty arises out of the relations in which men stand, the correct perception of it is dependent on a true knowledge of all the relations concerned. Each special relation develops its own moral obligation. Every set of circumstances imposes its peculiar moral demands. What is right in some relations is wrong in others. But the point to be observed, as the proof of the enthronement of a moral law within man, is that however men may vary in the judgments which apply it, they never for a moment doubt, or can doubt, that the law of right should in fact be applied. Amid all the differing judgments of conscience, it still judges; and the one judgment that is never withdrawn and from which there is no dissent, is the supreme authority of the moral idea or ethical law.

Secondly, like every other power of the mind, it is capable of different degrees of development. We have no mental faculties independent of training. They are all dependent on their right education for their true action and full service. They are often left almost wholly incompetent for their office. Mankind exhibit stages of development from the brutish degradation of savage tribes to the fine discriminations of the Christian philosopher. Ignorance of the realities of nature and the true relations of life, of the constitution of the world and of the laws which express its principles and purposes, must necessarily affect the correctness of men's perceptions of duty. Since obligations are developed by relations, ignorance or misapprehension of these cannot but confuse the application of the ethical law. Conscience can apply its intuitional distinctions only in the light that is afforded it in the knowledge enjoyed. In this part of its work it is by no means infallible. It would be exceedingly absurd to suppose that in the aggregate of man's finite and fallible faculties, this one should be asked to be, in its entire office under all conditions of mental development, above the possibility of being misled. When the fogs of ignorance darken and chill the whole soul, or when the general faculties of information have given error instead of truth, as to the facts in human life and its relations, the conscience must be almost helpless in discriminating the practical application of the principle of rectitude. It must have light. It must have its proper development. But still—and this is the point to be observed—the conscience, even in its most misguided judgments, continues to assert a necessary law of distinction between right and wrong, and of the legitimate supremacy of the right. In the very structure of his constitution man is framed into a moral system. He finds himself amenable to a law which is not the product of his will, but which is irrevocably imposed upon him as supreme for all his choices. All this testifies to the existence of a Lawgiver writing the high imperatives to righteousness and duty in man's inmost nature.

(4) Man's moral nature thus connects him with a moral system established by the determining cause of all. The reasoning is well put by Thomas Erskine: "When I attentively consider what is going on in my conscience, the chief thing forced on my notice is, that I find myself face to face with a purpose—not my own, for I am often conscious of resisting it, but which dominates me and makes itself felt as ever present, as the very root and reason of my being.... This consciousness of a purpose concerning me, that I should be a good man, right, true, and unselfish, is the first firm footing I have in the region of religious thought; for I cannot dissociate the idea of a purpose from that of a purposer, and I cannot but identify this purposer with the Author of my being and the Being of all beings; and further, I cannot but regard His purpose toward me as the unmistakable indication of His own character."

We may put this proof, in brief, in this way: Human personality is not of itself. It is notoriously limited, has a beginning, developing out of darkness into time and space, gradually waking up to self-consciousness and self-government; and plainly has not prescribed for itself the laws of its being—this law of moral obligation. It finds it in itself as given. The law of duty in the ethical perception, the imperative to right, must come from a source back of itself, binding human freedom to righteousness. The law, therefore, necessarily points back to the creative power that, as Lawgiver, has wrought it into man's constitution and evermore reveals through it His existence and sovereignty.

2. *From the existence of a moral administration over the world.* The evidences of this are found in the history of men and nations and the experiences of human life. It is universally admitted that by an established relation between actions and their

consequences the movement of the natural system of the world becomes a government of men by law. Consequences are not fortuitous, or in chaotic series, but are so united to their causes that they may be anticipated, and so either incurred or avoided.

They thus become rewards and punishments—foreannounced penalties directing men to that which will give them welfare and happiness. It is indisputable, also, that this natural administration is fundamentally *moral—i.e.,* its principle is to reward the right and punish the wrong. It is not maintained, indeed, that the world exhibits this moral administration in complete form or a perfect adjustment of recompense to virtue or vice. That is not the fact as actually observed. Righteousness is not always seen fully rewarded, nor crime justly punished. We cannot affirm, from observed facts alone, that this world shows a perfect moral government. Indeed, by reason of our but limited view of the relations of moral agents and their actions, we are incompetent to decide on the perfection of such administration. But what is unquestionable is that it presents an essentially moral system in the interest of righteousness.

This is practically involved and secured through the moral nature given to man. By the force of this every man is necessitated to hold himself and others as under obligation to truth, justice, love, and all the great principles of righteousness. Thus a moral force is at once started and enthroned for the regulation of individuals and society. This force from conscience is met by the objective moral relations of which it is adapted to secure the fulfilment. It is a most impressive fact, too, that the natural law of cause and effect has been so adjusted as to reward good action and punish deeds of vice. The virtuous emotions are made happy; those that are vicious are made painful. Wrong deeds wound the personal constitution; good ones improve and strengthen it. In the inter-human relations this law of effect is, with equal clearness, arranged on the side of righteousness. The whole system of human government and law, which is part of the natural system, is framed into the moral conception. Society punishes vice because it is injurious, and rewards virtue because it is beneficial. These effects make it the interest of society to favor righteous conduct *as* such, and to repress wrong as essentially undesirable.

Thus, though recompense is not found meted out perfectly according to deserts, yet the administration of the world is plainly seen to be on the side of right. Whatever imperfections may appear, there is not the faintest evidence to show that it is any part of the plan of the world's government to punish what is good because it is good, or to give advantages to wrong because it is wrong.

The moral constitution of the world, with an administrative organization on the principles of moral law, is well mirrored in history. Responsibility is one of the most comprehensive, serious, indubitable facts disclosed in the records of the race. It has turned history into drama, exhibiting crimes and criminals coming under judgment. Its startling realities led the ancients to enthrone a Nemesis for the earth. They have led thoughtful minds to speak of "God in History." So clearly do the conscience and the realities of a moral system reveal a moral governor, that even those who are inclined to break away from commonly accepted truth and hide a personal God from view or recognition, are yet constrained to concede the necessary existence of "the enduring power, not ourselves, which makes for righteousness." That this "power" cannot be simply a fortuitous "stream of tendency," as it has been called, is evident from the discriminating way in which the tendencies of actions are adjusted to the moral principle, good effects from right, and punitive from bad, deeds. At best, "tendencies" express only an observed order of effects, and the real "power that makes for righteousness" must be in an ordaining cause behind the effects. The moral principle on which the administration proceeds reveals a Moral Governor.

3. *From the relation between the moral law and the happiness of men.* This form of the moral evidence was developed by Kant, and was felt by him to be adequate ground for belief in the existence of God. The moral law is viewed as an original and unconditional command, manifesting itself within men as a "*categorical imperative.*" Its authority is established in its own command. The recognition of this authority appears as a sense of *duty*. Man finds himself under obligation to the moral idea. The reasoning may be

put into brief form as follows: We evidently exist for two ends—morality and happiness. We are bound to the moral law by an imperative that allows no dissent. It commands formally, irrespective of all consequences. We are also bound to happiness, by adaptations, desires, and capacities for it. Beyond our *own* happiness, this moral law obliges us earnestly and steadily to seek the happiness of others, as the chief natural good appointed for them. But these two ends to a great degree fail to coincide. They are not found to be in such practical harmony as to allow full realization and success in both directions. We find ourselves powerless to reach the aims that our nature imposes on us. Following the behests of the moral law, we fall short of gaining for ourselves and others the happiness for which nature has adapted men. Hence we are compelled by an act of moral faith or the practical reason to assume the existence of a moral Author and Governor of the universe and a future state, for an ultimate reconciliation of the appointments that appear in our nature. This is required to justify the moral imperative, as not commanding in contradiction of man's chief good.

These three distinct lines of reasoning from the aggregate of facts in the moral constitution concur to the same conclusion. The reality of the moral system is too large a phenomenon in the world, and exhibits too impressively the working of an intelligent purpose toward the loftiest ends of human excellence and welfare, to be attributed either to chance or simply physical law. The sphere of its results is one lifted too high above the range of material movement and relations to be explained except in connection with a rational system whose laws come from an ordaining moral Intelligence. Science knows of no properties of matter, no collocation of atoms, as equivalent to the moral idea and the imperative to righteousness. It has discovered no "potencies" of mere matter for the *origination* of the ethical law, so high above the grade of its blind interactions—this law of the sphere of freedom out of a sphere that knows no freedom. No satisfactory solution of the great facts of the moral system, in which man comes to his crown in the possibilities and requirement of moral worth, has yet been given or appears possible, except in the predetermining creatorship of a righteous God.

Here we close this brief survey of the natural evidences of the existence of God. It remains only to summarize them, so as to bring them in a connected view.

1. A very strong presumption of the divine existence arises from the universality of some idea of God, forcing itself, in some form or other, into the belief of all ages and all tribes; from a like universal religious instinct, showing a natural and profound adjustment of the human constitution to worship, a deep necessity for God in the aptitudes of man's soul; from the benign influence of this belief upon human life, quickening its sense of duty and responsibility, and supplying, in proportion to the correctness and strength of the faith, the motive force for the best development of man's noblest characteristics and interests; and from the fact that all the phenomena and mysteries of the world are best explained on the assumption of the existence of God. It is the only rational solution known for many of the most prominent phenomena—the most rational solution for all. On the scientific principle which holds a theory verified when it solves all the facts, the existence of God becomes thoroughly accredited.

2. The necessities of ontological thought afford another approach to this conclusion. We have an unavoidable knowledge of real existence or being, in our own consciousness of self and of objective nature. We have also an idea of God, or a divine existence, so spontaneous and normal as to be, in truth, a necessary idea. To think the thought of God fully and rationally, however, requires us to think of Him as an absolute or self-existent being. Our knowledge of real existence also compels us to believe in self-existent or eternal being. For, knowing that something now exists, it is impossible to deny that something has always existed. And thus our necessary rational thought of God as a self-existent being directly fulfils this ontological necessity of a self-existent being. This line of reasoning, however, does not in itself rigidly exclude pantheism, or make clear and certain the distinction between God and the universe itself. But the further evidences fully cover this point.

3. The cosmological inquiry, finding nature in all its parts and as a whole both finite and dependent, is compelled, under the law of causation, to assume an adequate cause for it all. The supposition of an absolutely eternal series of limited and dependent causes and effects is utterly excluded by its being a contradiction in terms. In searching back for the cause in this series of effects, the demand of the law of causation can never be satisfied until a cause is reached which is not itself an effect; that is, until a First Cause, a Self-existent, Absolute Cause is reached. This draws the line clearly between self-existent being and all dependent or begun being. If, therefore, the law of causation is true for the real system of things, this finite and dependent universe must demand an independent or self-existent cause. By an inexorable law of thought, Absolute Being is the correlate and basis of dependent being.

An absolutely *first* cause, one that is an *originating* force for effects, must be a *free* cause; and no realm of free causation is known except in Mind. This already, in cosmological evidence, points to the First Cause as a Rational Will. This evidence, therefore, not only requires a self-existent First Cause for the universe, but forbids all confounding of that Cause with nature itself, or any simply impersonal force.

4. The teleological feature that pervades all nature adds overpowering emphasis to the demand for an intelligent Creator. This characteristic, appearing not only in the order and useful adjustments of the universe in its aggregate balance and general movement, but in its myriads on myriads of distinctly adapted organisms, in wonderfully provided perpetuity of succession, in which are found, everywhere, the most discriminating predeterminations to sentient welfare and enjoyment, and especially in the purposive action of the whole mental realm in which nature's order or gradation comes to its consummation and crown, and receives its interpretation—this characteristic demands for its solution not only a cause, but an adequate cause, an intelligent cause, one of inconceivably great wisdom and power. The principle of design is seen to be coextensive with the highest law of the universe. The world appears as a thought, with evidences of purpose or intent shining all through it, from its

adapted atoms, acting like purposely "manufactured articles," up through all the aggregations in which these atoms form the cosmos. The correlate of all this thought is a Thinker as the Maker of the world.

It may be admitted that since the world or even the universe, however great, is still finite, it does not in itself and directly prove an absolutely *infinite* being. No finite product can, under the simple principle of causation, demonstrate an infinite power. This is freely conceded. But the value of the argument remains practically the same. For it is quite sufficient for all that is sought from it for theistic truth, when it proves the existence of an intelligent Creator of the actual universe. The question whether we dare speak of Him as "the Infinite" raises no practical difficulty. The theistic inquiry is, primarily, after a divine personal First Cause of the universe—our Maker and the Maker of all the worlds. It is enough that it is legitimate proof of this. Moreover, though the universe is indeed finite, yet as it is disclosed, especially in astronomical science, extending world on world, system on system, in countless constellations through illimitable space, beyond all the boundaries that the telescope can discern or the imagination conceive, it is so great that we need not hesitate to accept as true God the Being whose thought and will has given it its existence and order. Especially since the *cosmological* proof, under the law of causation, demands for the sum of all dependent causes and effects an *absolute* First Cause, and ontological thought spontaneously and necessarily affirms the Absolute Being as also infinite.

5. The last form of evidence, taking up the highest range of facts which the constitution of the world presents, finds in them impressive confirmation of the theistic conclusion. The ethical law in conscience, and the moral administration disclosing itself in experience, observation, and history, show how the whole system of things culminates in an evident purpose in the welfare of man. The Creator is shown to be a moral Lawgiver and Ruler.

6. The theistic evidences are thus, in the fullest sense, cumulative. The conclusion rests not on one proof or one kind of proof. Pursuing the different lines of reasoning here presented, we find them at last uniting in the common conclusion. But these

are only a few of the possible lines of proof. That which is made testifies to its Maker from so many points of observation and under so many processes that the evidences are endless. They mutually support and strengthen each other. Their force is seen and felt not in viewing them separately, but in their combination. So nature speaks with thousands of voices—with not one positive voice of dissent. It is in this consilience of evidence that we get the proper theistic proof. It is when all voices are heard that we get the sublime testimony of the universe to its Creator.

Natural Theology

PART II

THE CHARACTER OF GOD—HIS RELATION TO THE UNIVERSE

NATURAL Theology, as stated in the beginning of this discussion, includes an inquiry into the character of God, so far as this may be known from reason and nature. This part of the subject is here reached. It divides itself into two branches—the *essential attributes of the Deity,* and *His relation to the universe.*

CHAPTER I

THE ATTRIBUTES OF DEITY

THE inquiry into the divine attributes is an inquiry into those essential qualities or properties by which He is indeed God. The various evidences that show *that* God is, show also to some degree *what* He is. The divine attributes, therefore, are those characteristics by which the being or essence of God is distinguishable from all being that is not God. They are not to be understood as mere conceptions of our own which we attribute to God, but as realities in the divine nature and activity. Our reason does not create them, but apprehends them as they are disclosed and reflected from the same sources which prove His existence. Most of these attributes have already become evident by the facts which exhibit Him as the Creator and Lawgiver of the universe. A brief account of them will, therefore, suffice.

I. SELF-EXISTENCE

This means that His being is in Himself alone, underived and absolute. It denies origination, or dependence on prior being. Our idea of self-existence comes out of our analysis of the idea of being: Something is, therefore something has always been; and if something has always been, something must have been self-existent. The proof which shows that this necessary self-existence is found in God is given in the entire cosmological evidence. The law of causation demands, for the entire universe as finite and dependent, a cause which is not itself an effect. The First Cause is necessarily unoriginated.

II. ETERNITY

By this is meant that God neither begins nor ceases to be. This is directly involved in His self-existence. Since He is the unoriginated, absolute Being, there is no element of contingency in Him, and He is without beginning or end. He is the "necessary existence" from eternity to eternity.

III. PERSONALITY

The term "personality" covers several united attributes. In its complete import it denies that the First Cause is merely an unconscious, blind, non-intelligent force or principle, or that God is the impersonal sum of existence. He is a Personal Being. The elements of personality are reason or intelligence and free will or self-determination. A being that determines his own course in his own reason is a person. This, therefore, really includes these two attributes. *First, intelligence,* seeing its own way and the reasons of its own purposes; and *secondly, free will,* making and executing its own choices. As a person, therefore, God is the Rational, Self-determining Energy, the Supreme Reason and the Supreme Power.

The proofs of this personality begin in the ontological evidence which shows that if we think the idea of God rationally we must think of Him as the Most Perfect Being. This is found in no rank below free intelligence. The proof is strengthened through the conclusion of the cosmological reasoning, which discovers a First Cause only in mind as an originating will-force. It is confirmed by the whole force of the teleological evidences which show the world to abound in unmistakable marks of adaptive thought, requiring intelligence and will in the power that has made it. Especially is it proved by the grand phenomena which appear at the summit of this creation, the facts of human mind, with its intelligence, freedom, and moral law. Is it possible to conceive of the originative cause of human personality, with all its lofty realities, as itself something less than a person? Can this human intelligence be due to a cause that has none? This reason to unreason? This personality to impersonality? As easily may we think of something born out of nothing. Human mind is the proof of the divine mind. The myriad personalities that people the earth and time mirror the self-existent personality of the Power from which the world has come.

This accords with the fact that rational will is the synonym of originative *power*. Will is essential energy. Our very idea of power comes out of our consciousness of ourselves as exercising will-force. Of *originating* power we have no conception at all apart from personality. *Mind* stands to us as the synonym of genetic force. It is, therefore, with great reason that many of the acutest thinkers have always regarded all the force that appears in the processes of the universe as the movement of will-power. The efforts of scientists to show matter itself to be intrinsic and essential energy have not proved satisfactorily successful. The irresolvable *inertia* that everywhere marks it is greatly in the way of the attempt. But even should it be so maintained, matter, by the peculiar properties of its atoms, appears to be a constituted existence and must have its attractions and repulsions from the will of the Maker. Nature's forces manifest themselves as modes of motion; but the fountain of the power is discoverable only in the rational will in which the self-existent Being is both efficient and final cause for the creation of the universal system. Personality, therefore, is one of the great essential attributes of God. This is the truth about which, in a peculiar degree, all correct theism turns. As human personality is the supreme fact in man's nature, the one in which he comes into free power and all his highest distinctions, so the divine personality is preeminently that in which God is the Highest Perfection of being.

IV. SPIRITUALITY

This is closely allied to personality. It concerns the *essence* of God, and includes both a denial and an affirmation. It denies that He is matter; it affirms that He is Mind or Spirit. Intelligence, reason, will, are known to us only as functions of mind. The same evidences that sustain belief in His personality are evidences of His spirituality. He is the absolute Mind, whose thought and purpose illuminate the movements of the universe.

V. UNITY

God is one and alone. This means that He is not one of a class. There is not another to constitute a class. Each man is numerically one, and has the unity of a personal existence. But there are many individual men. The unity affirmed of God is that He is one and alone. There is only one God.

The evidences of this unity come: 1. In the cosmological argument which demands an absolute *First Cause* for the world. An absolute First Cause must be one. 2. In the attribute of personality. A person is a unity. 3. In the unity of the universe. Everywhere, on earth and in all the astronomical systems, the forces, laws, movements, and order constitute a singing harmony. One thought pervades the universe as an immeasurable organism. All worlds seem to respond to the same law of gravitation. The light from distant bodies, through the spectrum, shows the same qualities. The unity of the universe proves the unity of the Thinker, of whose thought and will it is an expression. This unity of the structure of nature may, indeed, be said to prove only a unity of counsel. And on the principle of simple induction from the unity of nature, it must be confessed, it could reach no further. But viewed in connection with the preceding evidences, it carries strong confirmatory force.

VI. INFINITY

The term "infinite," in this connection, must not be confounded with "the infinite" of abstract thought, conceived as the necessary "correlate" of the finite. That is a concept, and stands for a conceptual existence. But the term here is not used to express a thought-product, but to designate an *attribute* of a real Being. It is properly negative in form and in idea, signifying *not finite, unlimited.* When we speak of God as infinite we mean that His being cannot be brought under any limitations of space or time, nor can any of His attributes be classed as finite. The word denies imperfection of any kind or in any respect. In this peculiarity of expressing a negative predicate, the word "absolute" is like the term "infinite." When we say of God that He is absolute, our affirmation is that He is not dependent on any other being for His existence, nature, or activity. He is absolute as the self-existent First Cause.

It would be a fallacious process to convert these negatives directly into positives. And yet, if we will think carefully, we will perceive that there is necessarily a positive content included in the conception of these relations or attributes, in that the terms only deny limitations. The positive content—of being or relations—underlies the denial of limitation, and is the recognized basis for the distinction pointed out in the attribute. Thus this negative attribute of infinity, asserted in view of already given proofs of the divine existence, warrants the positive conception of the full perfection of God's nature and power.

The natural evidence of this infinity comes both from the rational necessity of conceiving of God as the Perfect Being, and from the practical boundlessness of the universe, transcending the utmost reach of the imagination. As mirrored in the immensity of the universe, the Creator must be recognized as infinite.

VII. A GROUP OF ATTRIBUTES INVOLVED IN THE DIVINE PERSONALITY AS INFINITE

1. *Omniscience.* This expresses the action of the divine intelligence as infinite. God knows Himself and all created and possible being and relations. Our necessary conception of the knowledge of such an intelligence includes such features as these: (1) It is intuitive. God knows by an immediate view. Man must find truth through extended processes and hesitating inferences. An infinite intelligence sees it all at once and directly. (2) It is certain. There can be nothing probable to it. There are no *unknown* contingencies to bring in any element of uncertainty. (3) It must be infallible. Its directness and infinity exclude mistake.

2. *Omnipresence.* An infinite Being is everywhere. No limit of space can be set for Him. This omnipresence, in Natural Theology, rests not only on this necessary implication of thought, but also on the fact that "in every part and place of the universe with which we are acquainted, we perceive the exercise of a power which we believe, mediately or immediately, to proceed from the Deity." He may well be said to be wherever He is seen to be working.

3. *Omnipotence.* Power is an attribute of the divine Will to which no limits can be affirmed, so far as objects may come within His choice. He is omnipotent for whatever He wills. It is impossible for us, in view of other necessary divine attributes, to conceive of self-contradictions, wrong, or other things sometimes said to be impossible to Him, as ever coming within the range of His choice. But for the objects of His will His power is omnipotent. The creation and preservation of the universe are the expressions of this power. It is true, the creation of a finite universe cannot be held as calling for the exertion of an absolutely infinite power, yet before the impression of power this

universe gives to our minds, the term "omnipotence" stands fully justified.

4. *Illimitable Wisdom.* Wisdom means a quality somewhat different from knowledge, as it expresses the action of intelligence in choosing the best ends and accomplishing them through the proper means. Natural Theology affirms this attribute, as involved in the personality of the divine Being. In this personality He is the infinite Reason. This excludes the unreasonableness in which want of wisdom consists. Supreme reason is supreme wisdom. This attribute, as thus made apparent in the very conception of the divine nature, is reflected from all the impressive phenomena which have formed the ground of the teleological reasoning.

VIII. HOLINESS

By this word we express the character of God under a view required by all the facts of the moral evidence. It signifies that the divine Will is eternally and perfectly consonant with intrinsic righteousness, and that this principle of righteousness, under which the moral system of the world has evidently been constituted, expresses the unchangeably holy nature of the Creator. Our reason compels us to think of this as a necessary attribute of a perfect Being; and the ethical law, to which we find our nature inexorably bound, is justly regarded as reflecting the character of the Lawgiver to our moral faculties. God's nature is perfect moral excellence, and His free will is the action of eternal righteousness.

IX. GOODNESS

Love and benevolence are synonymous terms for this. The idea intended to be set forth is that God delights to communicate the highest good to His creation. Benevolence is wishing the well-being of all. Love is a disposition to do good. We speak of this as "goodness." Employing it to designate an attribute of God, we conceive of this goodness as perfect. But it is in connection with this attribute that the main theistic difficulties have been alleged and felt. For, amid the prevalent, clear, and assuring indications of the divine goodness, there are discernible various contradictory appearances; some of them of such positive character and complex relations as to constitute profound and positively insoluble problems. The endless strife between optimism and pessimism—asserting, on the one hand that the world is the best possible, and on the other, that it is the worst possible—is constant testimony to the grave difficulties which certain phenomena of the natural constitution offer for solution. And yet when the phenomena which suggest these difficulties are examined in their last analysis and broadest relations, enough of explaining light shines through them to render it credible that, could we understand them fully, they would be seen to be well chosen parts of a benevolent whole.

1. The evidences on which we affirm this attribute are chiefly these:

(1) The great ethical principle which, as enthroned in our nature, requires us to believe our Creator to be righteous and holy, involves also the necessity of His goodness. The law of love is embraced in the supreme law of righteousness and holiness. The conception of right, taken in its fullness, includes love. For love is part of our highest duty. It belongs to our supreme obligation. No man exhibits full moral excellence, if he malignantly seeks the misery of others or is selfishly indifferent to their welfare. The law of love is required by the law of right. In binding us to the law of good-will, our Creator has forbidden us to think of Him as indifferent to the principle of goodness. This principle is a completing element in righteousness itself. God's very righteousness, therefore, obliges us to think of Him as acting in love. Whatever may be the aspects which the constitution of things presents, our moral nature prohibits us from conceiving of Him as indifferent to the happiness of his creation or appointing its order without respect to its highest good. The whole force, therefore, of the moral argument for the proof of a righteous Lawgiver and Ruler, requires also this attribute of goodness.

(2) The *wisdom* of God, in our necessary conception of the infinite reason or the divine personality, compels us to believe in

His goodness. As wisdom is concerned with the choice of ends and the ways of their accomplishment, it precludes the choice of either moral or physical evil as an end. It excludes all want of goodness from its action. Want of goodness is actual unreasonableness. Infinite wisdom cannot be in league with malevolence. Infinite reason cannot but prefer the happiness of creatures rather than their misery. The wisdom of God requires His love.

(3) The general tenor of the arrangement, order, and organization of creation clearly testifies to His goodness. The prevailing action of undisturbed, unperverted nature is good, and reveals a benevolent intention. Goodness, as well as wisdom, is seen in the exact adaptation of all the parts of our physical organization to their place and office in the composite structure; in the adjustment of the entire organism to the surrounding world; in the fitting of the body to the nature and service of the mind; and in the precise suitableness of the mental faculties to the ends of physical, intellectual, and moral well-being. Bounteous provision is made for the needs and happiness of all sentient existence, and the world abounds in happy life. Everywhere there is "a felicitous fulfilment of function in living things," and an exuberance of means of enjoyment is poured around all conscious being.

What is specially to be observed, as Paley has justly pointed out, is that "the Deity has superadded *pleasure* to animal sensations, beyond what was necessary for any other purpose, or when the purpose, so far as it was necessary, might have been effected by the operation of pain." Nourishment might have been supplied without the pleasure provided for in the specialized organs of taste. Motion might have been left unattended by the exhilaration and enjoyment it actually supplies. Every function of animal life, in uninjured and healthy condition, goes on, not only painlessly, but with a positive pleasure as something beyond the merely functional requirement. In the adaptations of the *human* constitution this feature is peculiarly distinct. It is a large fact in our happiness every day. All our special senses have been filled with this "superadded" good. Beginning with the fundamental form of touch, each sense-perception serves for pleasure in addition to utility. Through hearing and sight particularly, enjoyment is poured richly into every human experience.

But, highest of all, the constitution of the *mind* shows this benevolent intent. The intellectual powers exhibit a marvelous adaptation to the discovery of useful and gladdening truth. The reality and value of this adjustment are seen in the affluent treasures of general knowledge and science which have put all the experience of the past and the varied mighty forces of nature at man's service for utility and happiness. The triumphs of mind in the realm of modern knowledge have been magnifying the evidences of the divine goodness in constituting the powers of the intellect. In the emotional nature another realm of enjoyment is provided—the rich realm of love, friendship, the endlessly varied attachments of human souls in the fellowship of life. No one can think of the pure sweet joy thus provided and given to the world, without seeing that love opened this fountain. The human sensibility is a special provision for pleasure. Had this been made a blank, life would be poor indeed. Through the intellect and the emotions moreover, the Creator has furnished a distinct perception and appreciation of the beautiful with which the universe of nature is everywhere adorned. This lofty æsthetic endowment looks like a provision made solely for the sake of enjoyment, an unnecessary outburst of the Creator's kindness. And over against it, as a gift correspondent to the inner faculty, is an illimitable range of provided beauty in the world, from the beauty of the snowflake, the crystal forms of frozen moisture on a window pane, or the petals of the way-side flower, to the beauty of the starry sky or the symmetry of far-off cosmic systems. The poetry of all ages and lands has tasked its powers and tried its highest arts in attempts to express this universe of beauty and delight. There seems to be no end for beauty at all except the improvement and happiness of the rational creation. In the constitution, also, of the human powers into free personality and moral agency, and the organization of the race under moral law, the benevolent purpose is conspicuously clear. For it is only by an orderly fulfilment of the proper offices in the inter-human relations between the individuals of the race that man can reach his highest good, whether that good be viewed as consisting in character or happiness, or in both in indivisible union. That in every man's conscience, as the summit point of his nature, there is inscribed an imperative to righteousness and love, is, indeed, a crowning evidence of the Creator's benevolent aim.

Thus, everywhere through creation, in the minutest structures and most extended relations, these adaptations and provisions are found coordinated not only to necessities, but to further and distinct ends of welfare and enjoyment. They are not simply "conditions of existence," but clear provisions for happiness. These things have, in all ages and in every place, struck and impressed thoughtful minds as reflecting the goodness of God.

2. But the *difficulties* in the way of this broad conclusion must be stated. We do not include in these the existence of moral evil or sin, for the reason that this is produced by man's perverse use of his freedom, and exists only by contradiction of the divine will, as testified in the conscience. The position in which moral evil thus stands, as condemned and forbidden by the highest law the Creator has put in man's reason, makes it at least as available for the vindication as for the questioning of His goodness. But the evils which perplex us here are the *natural evils* which appear in the constitution of things.

The difficulties are such as these:

(1) Organisms are not all perfect. Many of them are of low order, put together apparently without much regard to convenience or comfort. They are deficient in strength and vital force. At best they are liable to derangement from accident or age.

(2) The adjustment between organisms and environment is not absolutely perfect. This is so with respect to man as well as the lower animals. There are antagonisms in the material forces that smite in injury, disease, and death. The air carries poisons as well as health. The food that is taken from Nature's hand often covers the cause of pain. At best, the physical powers without, which embrace and support the organism, often beat upon it in pitiless disregard of its comfort, and it is only a question of time when they will lay it in the dust. The friendly relation of the environment is not unqualified. The adaptation is not perfect.

(3) Even as to physical nature itself the world presents some features which do not seem to be the best possible. It is girdled with zones either painfully hot or distressingly cold; it has vast tracts of barren desert or wastes of rocks; it is shaken by destructive earthquakes and burned with outpoured subterranean fires; it is swept by tempests and beaten by the lightnings and hail of the sky. The air is loaded often with miasma and carries the pestilence on its wings. These and like things are alleged as proof that the world has not been made with either perfect wisdom or perfect goodness. It has been arranged, it is sometimes claimed, in reckless disregard of the safety, comfort, and happiness of the sentient creation.

(4) But the chief arraignment of the goodness of nature's determining cause has been drawn from the existence in it of an order of warfare of life on life. We are pointed to indisputable facts which show that from the earliest animal life, traceable by geology, till now the earth has been a scene of death and carnage. Living creatures have always been pursuing and devouring one another. Many of the organs whose structure the naturalist so justly admires are simply offensive and defensive arms, instruments of attack and resistance. To a large degree life is kept up by death, and through the violence of prey. In each of the great classes of animals there are some species that feed on others. There are insects of prey, reptiles of prey, fishes of prey, and quadrupeds of prey. They are provided with instruments of seizure and slaughter. We find the skilfully adapted talon, and fang, and poison. The continuance and progress of animal life on the earth seems thus to be a triumph of power over helplessness, a survival of the strongest, not alone as against the inanimate force of environment, but in this ceaseless battle for food. Man himself carries on the system—killing for his food whatever animals suit his taste. From the worm up to man is seen the great law of the violent destruction of living creatures. It seems to have been organized into the plan of nature.

3. It may not be possible to clear up all difficulties on this subject, but the following considerations will go far toward relieving them.

(1) There may be both wisdom and goodness in arrangements which yet fail to show *perfect* wisdom and goodness. Were it proved that the distribution of heat and cold, land and water, rocks and deserts and fertile plains, now marking the condition of the earth, is not the very best, it would not thereby be shown that there is no wisdom or goodness at all in it. Every creature in the world and every provision on earth is finite, and the finite must always have *some* limitations. It is always possible to conceive of something more perfect than any finite thing. A finite good may yet be a real good.

As to the order of the physical world and the grade of organisms, this asserted defect is in truth but relative perfection. We dare not translate it into terms of suffering or a ground of complaint, unless we deny the right of the finite to exist. Moreover, the thing complained of may be found to serve a positive good. The Alpine glaciers which encumber vast tracts of land are found to contribute irrigation and fertility to the far-off valleys. The mountains which, with their wilderness of cliff and forest, withdraw so much of every continent from the use of the husbandman, are, however, important factors in directing the atmospheric currents, distributing the showers of the sky, breaking the force of storms, and spreading some gifts from sea to sea. In respect to arrangements in the sphere of material existence, we need to be careful lest our hasty judgments foolishly deny relative or limited good to be good at all.

(2) There may be both wisdom and goodness *where we can see neither*—where, indeed, there seems to us to be the contrary. For we are very imperfect judges of a system so vast as this universe—filling such space, progressing through such eons. Butler, in his great *Analogy*, has long taught men the rashness and folly of dogmatically criticizing either the part or the whole of this imperfectly comprehended scheme. The science of every year is but throwing the boundaries of the universe into wider and more untraceable relations, and while adding to our knowledge, adding also to our conviction of the transcendence of these relations. We can survey but a very small part of this universe of world-systems and nature's progress, and understand only imperfectly the little of it that we do see. The parts we see

are so related to the past and future, and are so connected in their probable bearings on what is beyond our vision, that we really see nothing in its wholeness or completeness. We see but fragments in half-vision or imperfect vision, so that we are very liable to mistakes when we venture to sit in judgment on the order or plan or wisdom of the creation. Could we survey it all, and comprehend the complex relations of every part to every other part, and of all to the whole system, such explaining light might be shed upon it all that what is now dark and perplexing might become a bright reflection of wisdom and love.

Perhaps it will be said in reply to this, that if we are incompetent to declare things to be evil, we are also incompetent to declare things to be good. But the two sides are not equal, because it is indisputable that the world abounds in natural good, and that the evil is exceptional; for this is a matter of experience. Indeed, according to the prevalent conception of the survival of the fittest, a system preponderatingly evil could not perpetuate itself through the ages. Progress is said to be necessarily in the line of that which is most desirable; that is, of natural good. The thought of our day, therefore, concedes that natural good is ascendant in nature. It is reasonable, therefore, under these circumstances, not, indeed, to deny the existence of evil, but to believe that, could we interpret everything in the light of perfect knowledge, we would find goodness in many things in which we now fail to discover it.

(3) "In by far the greater number of contrivances in which design is seen in nature, the design is clearly perceived to be *beneficial.*" No one needs any other evidence of this than that which presses on him when he looks within him and around him, and faces the thousands of beneficent adaptations filling the world with comfort and happiness. That the prevailing order of nature, and the specific purpose and action of nearly all organisms, and parts of organisms, are beneficent, is beyond question. They are found to be actually adapted to serviceable and useful ends. Nine hundred and ninety-nine out of every thousand functions clearly show a purely kind intent. This overwhelming proportion must be considered as fairly declaring the Author of nature to be benevolent. The presumption becomes,

therefore, exceedingly strong that the one which carries some perplexing relations is not really, but only apparently, inconsistent with His goodness.

(4) In no place where suffering or pain is found in connection with an organism does it appear that *pain, for its own sake, is the object of the contrivance.* It comes as incidental to the attainment of the design. There may be pain from having teeth, but there is no evidence that teeth were created for the purpose of aching. To a very large extent even the incidental sufferings have been brought on by unnatural or artificial modes of life. It would, indeed, require a physical system of steel-like strength to bear unharmed and in painless integrity the perverse and violent treatment it receives even under our merciful civilization. The organizations are not for the sake of pain, but for the useful functions of life and enjoyment. Their healthy functions are pleasurable, and the suffering which comes with injury or decay only raises the question how far goodness must secure limited beings from such injury or decay. The pain, however, inflicted on others when animals simply act out the evident intent of their provided organization, as in their conflicts with one another, cannot, indeed, be interpreted as due to impaired function. Yet it, too, stands as incidental. There is pain from the wasp's sting, the viper's poison, the eagle's talons, the horse's hoof; but both the structure and the instincts which employ the structure in these cases look directly to the ends of defense and self-preservation. We know of no case in which provision is made for the infliction of suffering for its own sake. The ends which these perplexing organs actually serve, and which we must suppose they were meant to serve, are of the highest value to the animal's own existence.

(5) The whole difficulty, therefore, so far as concerns the order of life below man, is reduced to the fact of *animal death, especially in the system which includes their feeding upon one another.* The other points of objection, as limitations of natural good, are not found to be in direct and necessary contradiction to the divine goodness. But the considerations that relieve our minds as to them fall short of being a satisfactory explanation here. Whether or not a full solution can be given, the following

circumstances are to be taken into account: (*a*) Physical death, after all, being but another expression for temporary life, is in truth only a further feature of the limitation of finite existence. It is but the boundary to which the natural good is extended. That the life is not made everlasting is no disproof of goodness. (*b*) The life of animals of any species whatever, in the duration given it, is in the main a life of positive pleasure. Unquestionably the amount of physical enjoyment far surpasses the incidental pains that befall them. (*c*) These incidental pains come out of the same sensitive organization by which they have their capacities and experiences of enjoyment. They are a reversal of the action of their constitutional endowments for pleasurable sensations. (*d*) A system which would exclude death, would, by necessarily making each given life everlasting, almost infinitely diminish the number of individual animals that could exist and enjoy life. Under the limitation assigned to individual lives, new generations are forever coming into an existence of enjoyment, and the sum of animal enjoyment is, probably, much increased by this succession of generations. If the animal life is to be considered as counting for a pleasure at all, and goodness is at all concerned in the gift, this goodness is not necessarily impeached by the order which limits individual duration in the interest of this endless multiplication of numbers through endless succession. (*e*) The further feature of the system, by which the different species of animals become food for one another, appears to be part of this order under which such multiplication of individuals is incalculably extended. In the perpetual provision of food in this way, in addition to the supply in vegetable form, there is allowed a more rapid and numerous increase, in all the ranks from the lowest to the highest. The vacated space is quickly filled. The process by which the living have food is a process by which still more come to live, and the sum of animal enjoyment is made greater. (*f*) As to the termination of life in this sudden and violent way, it is by no means certain that the sum of animal suffering is thus increased beyond what it would be if life ended only by the slow exhaustion and decay of the organizations. We have, indeed, no reason to suppose animals incapable of pain, even great pain, but most of them are, without doubt, of far duller nervous organization than ourselves, many of them probably of very slight sensibility, and all of them without any rational conception or fear of death; and we must not fall into the illusion which measures death to them in the measures of human shrinking and sensibility. The instinctive action of timidity and flight, by which they avoid danger, may possibly understand itself as little, and be as destitute of real suffering, as other instinctive forces which blindly act for self-preservation. Without pressing these facts to any extreme, there is unquestionably some abatement to be made from the notion often formed of the suffering experienced in the lot of the lower animals, especially in connection with their death. At any rate, the supposed horrors of fear and apprehension attributed to them are probably largely phantoms projected from our human experience, and without reality for the experiences and acts of their automatic instinct. When their lives are thus ended suddenly, the pain, probably of quite inferior grade, is but for a moment. The slow action of age and weakness, with protracted discomfort, is excluded.

These various considerations may not, indeed, remove all our perplexity in the face of this feature of nature. Though diminished it is not gone—nor turned into genuine satisfaction. Something of mystery, it must be confessed, still shadows the fact as it presses itself on our view. Nor ought we to be surprised at this. For the immense sweep of nature's plan extends so far beyond our vision that the explaining facts and relations, though real, may be out of sight. A broader and deeper knowledge might turn our remaining perplexity into entire and positive satisfaction.

There is a peculiar fact that is, probably, worthy of notice and remembrance in this connection. The thing which so much offends, and disturbs faith in the divine goodness, ceases to offend just where we come into practical relation to the system. Men who object to the scheme of nature which includes the death of animals for food, have no convictions against it when they themselves are in free and voluntary identification with the scheme. The system comes to its fullest measure in man's use of animal food. If it violates goodness in its beginnings, it violates it when perfected. Man slays and appropriates from the whole animal kingdom whatever he can use for his needs and enjoyment. He heads the class of carnivora. And the singular thing is that while he is following this course in the freedom of his own choice, and in the presence of his moral sentiments, he shows no signs that he either judges or feels his chosen course as intrinsically or in its very nature wrong. That which so perplexed him when looked at from afar, among fish, and birds, and quadrupeds, when offered to personal use is judged and freely accepted as useful and good. His appreciative feeling prompts him even to natural gratitude to the Author of nature for the goodness that thus furnishes all that adds to the enjoyments of his life.

We do not recall this relation of men to this system of nature, and the silence of their consciences in their voluntary participation in it, as any positive answer to the objection which we are considering. It is not proved right by an appeal to their compromise with it. Man's acceptance of the system as good for himself falls short of a proof of its absolute goodness. But we call attention to it for the purpose of reminding that the standpoint from which we view a feature of nature may have much to do with our capability of judging of its wisdom or goodness. Our judgments are modified by our points of observation, affording us different degrees of light for correct conclusion. In the relation in which man knows most about this perplexing phenomenon, he objects to it the least. It is hardly consistent for him to hold it as irreconcilable with goodness when he approves of it in his own practice.

(6) *Pain and suffering* are not necessarily a disproof of the Creator's goodness. They may possibly stand in such relation to the whole system of things that they mark and exhibit its noblest exaltation. We must recall such things as these: (*a*) They may be part of the essential capacity for pleasure. Pleasure may be impossible except in an organization that at the same time allows pain. Liability to suffering may be an incident inseparable from sensitiveness. The nerve that was made to leap with pleasure may thereby become a channel to pain. With the gift of sensation rises the dawn of higher being in nature's ascent. (*b*) The office of pain is primarily good—to warn and restrain from what would injure

and destroy the organization. Insusceptible to pain, the organization would be wrecked. Prof. Flint well says: "Painful sensations are only watchful videttes upon the outposts of our organism, to warn us of approaching danger. Without these the citadel of our life would be quickly surprised and taken." (*c*) Pain is a stimulant to exertion, and it is only through exertion that life has health and development. The uncomfortable sensations of hunger or thirst are stimuli to action necessary to animal well-being. Life remains in lowest grades where there are no exercising forces of keen hunger or driving desire. The measure of sensitiveness becomes the measure of development and elevation of life.

In man, especially, where the heights of created existence on the earth are to be reached, where not only physical well-being, but intellectual activity and moral excellence are aimed at, the office of sensitiveness seems to stand as a lofty endowment, and its service as a training and perfecting force becomes conspicuous and great. Whatever unexplorable reason may underlie the plan in which such a method of development has been appointed to him, of the fact itself there can be no doubt. The disciplinary, educative, almost creative power of suffering is unspeakably great and valuable, and accomplishes, in character and welfare, unquestionably benevolent results. All the highest things in man's life, his developed self-control, energy, strength of virtue, kindness, beneficence, all the qualities which the world admires and extols as lifting human nature out of littleness and flatness into real grandeur, are gifts of the training in which the sharp experiences of pain and suffering have contributed their essential help. This method of development makes it clearly evident that there are loftier elements of well-being for man's nature and design than mere enjoyment or the placid repose of exemption from pain. Suffering is not a good in itself, but it fulfils a benevolent agency. And who can positively affirm that the constitution of the world, which permits it to enter as the attendant of the high grade of organization capacitating for pleasure, is a contradiction to the goodness of nature's author? For aught we know, the system may work out higher ends of being and blessedness than could otherwise be attained.

(7) It is worthy of consideration, also, that the liability to suffering comes naturally, and perhaps necessarily, under the action of *good and needed general laws*. From the earliest times in which men began to penetrate the method of nature, it has been understood to accomplish its results under the operation of fixed and uniform laws. Its forces and modes are established in the unity and harmony of a moving system fulfilling its ends age after age. The uncertainty and confusion of random occurrence are excluded. All events take place under orderly causation. Modern science has emphasized this uniformity of nature as the grand fundamental truth, on the basis of which all investigation must be carried on, and all its conclusions must rest. It is universally conceded that this orderly sequence in the ceaseless process from cause to effect, in fixed regularity, is the very beauty and strength of nature, the great principle which turns chaos into the cosmos. This uniformity of nature is the product of the uniformity of causation; and viewed in the light of theistic thought, this uniformity of causation is due to the creative and ordaining will of God. The reign of law, in this sense, is now recognized as covering the whole field of physical nature, from the movement of starry spheres to the fall of a sparrow or the coloring of a rose's petal.

This principle of law extends into the mental and moral worlds—the laws here being appropriate to the rationality and freedom which belong to these realms. The laws which express the modes of cause and effect in the material world, and those which belong to the higher range of intellectual and moral order, respectively, are peculiar to their own sphere and rank, yet they are adjusted to each other, and by their adjusted action, the universe becomes unified and harmonized under established general laws.

It is one of the great truths, now settled beyond all question, that this uniformity and permanence of law is the condition and basis, not only of all the order, strength, beauty, and glory of physical nature, but of all the possible excellence, success, and blessedness of human life. Because nature is fixed, human freedom can choose, and act with success. Laws, running their clear lines onward through every sphere, and showing results in advance, are the Creator's call and demand for obedience and conformity. They light up the future to our view and choices. Through this fixedness of linked consequence, seemingly so stern and merciless, we can look onward down the years and ages, and work out the highest possibilities in our nature and powers. It is only thus that nature is at all a subject of knowledge or science, or that its forces and movement are capable of being used by man. Only thus, indeed, could animal life, our own, or that of the lower orders, maintain itself at all. Only thus can we choose or carry out any choice. Only thus can there be responsibility or moral character, or any ends open to our attainment. Only thus can there be knowledge, business, art, industry, literature, civilization, and culture. Without this system of general and unbending law, so far as we can see, nature must return to chaos and the world cease to be a theater for the lofty things which belong to free intelligent personality. Though men have often arraigned the constitution of the world because of some severe consequences of such unbending action of physical and moral laws, this very feature is the condition of their being even able to understand enough of nature to be able to formulate their complaints. There can be no question that it bears abundant evidence of being essentially a scheme of wisdom and goodness.

Under such a system of general and uniform laws, opening up the possibility of all that is judged highest and best in being, it may not be possible to prevent or exclude all liability to suffering. The liability becomes a reality when the laws of nature and well-being are not observed but violated. The suggestion, made occasionally in past times, of immediate interpositions to prevent the consequences fixed in nature's laws of cause and effect, can plead no advantage for its plan. For, analyzed to the last, it involves the abandonment of the whole law of order. In the high range of human freedom, it would sink all the qualities of consideration, forecast, prudence, and care, and remove the basis and fact of responsibility and virtue, annulling all the discipline of intelligent power and moral character. It is by no means certain that the system of the world would be made better by insuring the safety and enjoyment of all creatures in recklessness, indifference, or inaction. If natural and moral laws were made few and uncertain; if their action were suspended whenever their ongoing would afflict anyone on their track; if fire would cease to burn whenever the helpless were exposed to it; if water would lose its essential qualities and refrain from drowning the crew of the wrecked vessel; i gravitation were to cease whenever anyone would be broken or crushed by its movement; if, in short, nature's forces should take an added law to stop whenever their uniformities would maim or wound anyone, it might indeed seem to be a very merciful or loving modification; but in view of some of the consequences which, we can see, would at once connect themselves with the new order, and others which may be wholly beyond our vision, it becomes exceedingly doubtful whether we can convict the principle of uniformity and inflexible order of want of wisdom or goodness.

(8) The final settlement of the question between optimism and pessimism, whether the world is the best world possible, or the worst, *is probably impossible from a simple observation and comparison of the facts of nature and experience.* These facts both reflect light and cast shadows, and their testimony as it comes to us needs an interpreter who stands on a higher point of view, and in a broader light than is possible to us here. The question must be answered rather from our necessary conception of the perfect nature of the Infinite Being. In the final response, the necessary character of God must explain the creation, and assure that, though some shadows lie upon it, it all together stands for a thought of wisdom and an aim of love. And, thus, the question calls for more light than reason and nature alone can give—the illumination of the Christian revelation. All that Natural Theology can settle at this extreme point—and it is enough that it can do this—is (*a*), that no suffering is found inflicted for its own sake; (*b*), that all the direct ends of nature are clearly beneficial and good; (*c*), that most of the perplexing features are really but defects implied in all creation as finite and limited, which we interpret into terms of suffering; and (*d*), both the general purpose of happiness unmistakably written on nature, and the very conception we necessarily have of God as the Perfect Being, the Perfect Reason and Wisdom, warrant the conclusion that goodness really presides over the aggregate scheme, and that,

could we understand it fully, the perplexing features would come under love's illumination, and cease to perplex.

Natural Theology

CHAPTER II

RELATION OF GOD TO THE UNIVERSE

THE inquiry here includes two distinct questions. The first is whether God is to be conceived of as transcendent to the universe or as immanent in it, or as in both these relations. The second is: What is the supreme or ultimate end in creation?

I. WHETHER TRANSCENDENT OR IMMANENT

It needs to be observed at the outstart that the existence of God, as shown by the evidences in the first part of this work, is a truth independent of the question here raised. That truth rests upon its own basis. Yet the proofs which have established it have the further force of opening the way to a right conclusion as to this additional question. The facts which have shown the existence of God shed light on His relation to the creation which appears as His work.

1. The entire evidence shows that God and the universe cannot be identified. For, on any philosophy capable of being applied to the theistic evidences, the Cause must be distinguished from the effect. To imagine the universe to be at once the cause and the effect of itself, would set at nought the logical demand of all the great facts in the case. These facts, especially in the cosmological and teleological evidences, forbid the idea that nature itself may be the absolute, eternal, self-existent being. It bears incontestable marks of dependence and origination. The pantheistic conception which makes God and the world one—

pantheistic monism—is clearly excluded by the necessary distinction which the principle of causation compels us to make between the cause and the effect. The Supreme Cause, that which is the Cause of all secondary or instrumental and dependent causes in nature, must be other than nature itself and distinct from it.

2. The relation between cause and effect, therefore, on which the proofs of the divine existence rest, requires us to conceive of God as *transcendent* in respect to the universe. The Cause is before and above the effect. This relation is part of the essential conception of the principle of causation. This transcendent relation of God as the Creator of the universe is universally admitted, except by the extreme materialism which denies His existence, or by the pantheism which identifies that existence with the universe, holding the physical universe as but the evolution of the divine substance. This pantheistic conception, however, when viewed in its last analysis, turns into atheism. For it finds no God other than the universe itself, the sum of nature.

In affirming this necessary transcendence of the Deity as thus demanded under the conception of Him as the First Cause of all, we must, nevertheless, avoid what has been called "absolute transcendence." Natural Theology has to guard against a false extreme. An "absolute transcendence" would regard Him as so separate from the universe as not to be in it or act in it, but as, after having created its substances and established its forces and laws, simply observing its ongoing, as an artificer might observe the movement of the mechanism which he has constructed. Such a notion of transcendence, found in some of the writers of ancient Greece and Rome, has often since reappeared. God was elevated to an empyrean far beyond the movement and noise of the world, and represented as wholly unconcerned about the vicissitudes and issues of life. This extreme view has too frequently affected theological thought and representation. The supermundane relation has been exaggerated into an almost impassable gulf. Neither prayer nor its answer can cross it. The creature is thrust outside of fellowship with the Creator. The system of nature is a mechanism constructed and wound up, to run of itself its fixed course. No such absolute transcendence is required, however, by the evidences here concerned. No such extreme separation should be included in our notion of the relation of the Deity to the world. Yet God must be before and above the universe of created existence. A real and essential transcendence is the first and fundamental requirement of all the evidences which prove Him to be the absolute Creator.

3. The same causal relation which thus necessitates our conception of the divine transcendence requires us to recognize also the divine *immanence* in the world. For the causal action did not remain external, acting only from outside of nature, but has become an omnipresence and power within it. God appears as essentially a transitive Cause, passing over and forever filling as well as abiding in the universe. All causes are the established onflow of the divine will and energy. They could not be, or continue, without Him. The universe is in God, and God in it forever, by necessity of His infinity and omnipresence. This truth resolves and harmonizes the difficulties suggested by the natural facts of immanent causation and finality. It neither denies nor obliterates the reality of second or physical causes and laws in nature, but recognizes their dependent relation to the purpose and establishing will of the absolute Creator. The fact of secondary causation, of efficient energy, under natural or fixed law, moving and developing as material and physical forces, is unquestionable, and not at all to be dropped from view. It is indeed the fundamental reality underlying the entire proof of the divine existence. The search in the whole inquiry of theism is after the cause of these natural powers and their established action. We, therefore, must not fall into the mistake of some theistic writers, who have attributed each separate and individual event in nature to a direct act of the divine will or energy. This error annihilates the reality of secondary causation. It is not only in plain contradiction of all that we know of the constitution of nature, whether as ascertained in common knowledge or through science, but it vacates the very postulate on which the theistic argumentation is based. Natural forces are real, and the laws of their action are made immanent in the nature of the elements or organism in which they show themselves. But they are the real products and ordinations of the will of the Deity who gave them

their reality and appointed their modes or laws. They remain as the permanent ordinary or natural powers, of divine creation and establishment. The laws of nature are modes of the divine power and will in nature; yet they have been fixed by the creative act within the very forces which exhibit them. They are the sequences according to which God ordinarily acts, yet their results come, not as direct, but as mediate products of the divine power.

The logical demand of the facts of the cosmic system point, therefore, to the conclusion that God, who was before the universe, not only created the natural forces, with their modes which we call laws, as real subordinate agents for their intended results, but that in His infinity He filled, and forever fills, the universe with His presence and power. The First Cause becomes transitive, and His presence is never separated from His power.

As it has been necessary to guard against an absolute transcendence, so it is needful to guard against an "absolute immanence." Rational theism must reject this error as well as the other. While an absolute transcendence would represent God as a remote Deity, keeping wholly outside of His works and giving it no presence or love or living relation to Himself, an absolute immanence would run into a pantheistic identification of God with nature itself, making the universe but an evolution of the substance of God. This error fails to maintain the distinction between God and nature, and in attempting to make all divine leaves nothing divine—loses God in an absolutely immanent cosmical causality. This absolute immanence of causality and finality, whether of the materialistic or the pantheistic sort, is one of the subtlest repudiations of true theism, and but another name for atheism. This transitive immanence, however, which starts with the recognition of the essential and necessary transcendence, maintains the proper and real dualism of God and nature, the Creator and the creation, and yet confesses His presence and power everywhere. It is in harmony with the conception of nature as a true effect of an originating Cause, and at the same time recognizes the unceasing and omnipresent working of God within and through it. As a conclusion of Natural Theology, it is also in harmony with the view of poets and sages of our Christian Scriptures, who looked on everything as God's doing. It is in consonance with the teaching: "In Him we live and move and have our being." He is above nature and below it, without it and within it, yet never a part of it. He is not nature, but nature is from Him and subsists by Him.

> "Super cuncta, subter cuncta,
> Extra cuncta, intra cuncta;
> Intra cuncta, nec inclusus,
> Extra cuncta, nec exclusus;
> Super cuncta, nec elatus,
> Subter cuncta, nec substratus;
> Super totus, præsidendo,
> Subter totus, sustinendo"

4. It is proper yet to emphasize what has been implied all along, that the relation of God is that of *absolute* Creator, and not an artificer working with eternally existent materials. The dualism of God and nature is not a dualism of two eternally existing substances, God and matter; but the relation in which Deity stands as the absolute Creator of the elements as well as the form of the world. The rational concept of God is that of the unconditioned ground of all being. This excludes the self-existence of matter—which would condition the divine activity. Moreover, if matter were eternal, its laws would not be of God, but inherent and beyond God. The whole basis of the universe would thus be outside of God. He would be reduced to simply a cunning and skilful architect. The notion of the eternity of matter has had a large place in the thought of past times, and remains to some extent in the present. Its old motto: *"ex nihilo nihil fit,"* is still quoted in its old sense. But when used in any other meaning than as a statement of the universality of the law of causation and of the necessity of postulating a First Cause of all things, it leads to an idea forbidden by the whole body of the theistic evidences. These evidences call for one absolute Being as the sole self-existence. And all that science has been able to show of material atoms and their combinations reveals a purpose, plan, or adaptation in their essential structure, as of manufactured articles, or subordinate and prepared agents. The entire

teleological evidence points clearly to Mind as the cause of the forces, laws, and products of matter. The orderliness of these forces and laws, their beautiful adaptation to the ends of intelligence and purpose, are inconsistent with the notion of their independent existence. Kant, in one of his earlier essays, well says: "There is a God, because nature, even in chaos, could not proceed otherwise than with regularity and order.... Left to its own general qualities, nature is rich in fruits which are always fair and perfect. Not merely are they harmonious and excellent themselves, but they are adapted to every order of being, to the use of man and to the glory of God. It is thus evident that the essential properties of matter must spring from one mind, the source and ground of all beings; a mind, in which they belong to a solidarity of plan."

This absoluteness of God's creative relation compels us to think of time and space as of God. Time and space are not to be thought of as entities or relations independent of Him and of His creative action, as they have often been represented. Nor are they mere subjective, illusive notions of our own minds, mere forms of thought, after the misleading doctrine of relativity in the Kantian philosophy. They are true for the actual universe. Yet they belong to the universe only as created by God. Space, in itself, is only the possibility of extended material existences. That possibility is only in the creative power of God. Apart from Him, space is absolute *vacuity,* utter nothingness. Time is the possibility of finite events or existences, with some continuance. Apart from God, time is nothing—only the possibility of something. These possibilities were originally only in God. Time and space, as conceived before the creation, can be conceived of only as the *not-being* of anything but God. When He creates beings other than Himself, time and space relations begin for the universe.

II. THE SUPREME OR ULTIMATE END IN CREATION

The law of ends, so clear and decisive in the constitution and relations of the various parts of nature, compels belief in an ultimate all-inclusive end. The teleological principle, once admitted, must be extended to the universe in its totality. There must be some supreme purpose to which all subordinate purposes converge and in which the relations of all are consummated. If God created the very substances with properties fitted for their intended service in world-building; and has given to each organism a complex of distinct adaptations to both internal uses and external conditions, if all nature is made a balanced order, a very cosmos, moving on in a steady harmony and rational progression, we are logically forced to conclude that He created the entire system of things for some defined and specific end. Nothing seems to exist for itself alone. The parts everywhere have relation to the whole. Everything looks to something beyond itself, and is framed into a grand system embracing the entire universe. The creation as such must stand for and express a purpose. Only thus does the law of ends find its full comprehension. Only thus is the origin of the universe in a designing Intelligence really and fully justified. This ultimate purpose expresses one aspect of God's relation to the world.

But what is that purpose? For what end did God give existence to the universe? Why did He create it? This question, it must be borne in mind, is different from the question whether He had any end. The reality of final cause in nature is always to be distinguished from our ability to discover the actual purposes. The existence of ends is one thing; our discovery of them is quite another. The interpretations which men have put on nature's organizations and relations have often been absurdly mistaken. Teleology has often been discredited by the grotesque blunders and frivolous explanations of its friends. It is one of the offices of true progressive science to enable us to read the thought of God more correctly in nature's specific structures and relations. While in many things, as in the eye or ear, the end is unquestionable, and it would be a spurious modesty of knowledge to affect not to know it, in others the ends are so obscure or complicated, or reach out into so wide a circle of relations, as to make the most skilful interpreter rightly hesitate to claim a full or certain knowledge of them. In so large a problem as that which seeks the supreme purpose of the universe itself, the ultimate aim to which it has been adjusted, our certainty that it has an end may not be equaled by our certainty of knowing it. The difficulties to our knowledge arise not alone from the vastness of the universe, stretching almost to infinity of space and time, but from the necessary limitations under which our finite minds must ever view the infinite thoughts and purposes of the Eternal Mind. Yet even here, guided by the truth that our reason is in the pattern of the Infinite Reason, our personality is in the mold of the Infinite Personality, we may find the light of truth shining with such clearness as to assure our confidence. We may probably know the generic end of the divine purpose in creation.

1. Several questionable views have been widely asserted. One is, that God created the universe *for Himself or His own glory*. The reasons alleged for this view are: (1) That before creation, God being the only and absolute Existence, the whole reason of creation, *i.e.,* both motive and aim, must have been in Himself. There was nothing else with respect to which He could act. (2) That, as He could act only for the worthiest object, one of infinite worth, He could find it only in Himself. His own glory could be the only worthy object. But the following considerations are enough to make us hesitate to accept this explanation: (1) That though the universe was not actually existent, it was existent in the divine thought and plan, and could thus certainly stand for an end in the divine action. (2) That it seems to imply that God was not absolutely self-sufficient, but was lacking something which He created in order to complete Himself or His glory. If it be maintained, as the theory appears to assert, that God can act only for an infinite object, and can have no end outside of Himself, creation becomes inexplicable; for, as already having Himself, why should he seek Himself in a roundabout way? If the terminus of the divine aim was absolutely Himself, how would he ever have come out of Himself in creative work? (3) It implies—and this is the decisive trouble in this theory—that the divine activity is necessarily, in its final aims, supreme self-seeking. Creation is made a selfish proceeding. It is impossible to save the theory from this implication. Even when it is shaped with a view to avoid it, the taint of the implication inheres in it. For if the ultimate end, that which subordinates everything else to itself, is His own glory, then all else falls into the relation of mere means, and love

becomes subordinate to self-aggrandizement. The infinite perfections of God, especially as unified in love, seem clearly to forbid this theory.

Another theory represents that God created for the sake of the *happiness of the creation*. It holds that though infinitely happy in Himself, He, out of pure goodness, desired to give existence and happiness to other and finite beings. But this view is defective for two reasons. (1) It goes on the assumption that simple happiness is the creature's supreme good. (2) It fails to take account of the ethical character of God, which must necessarily have place and manifestation in His creative will and plan. God may delight in creating excellence as well as happiness. In His sight there may be something higher than enjoyment. The great ethical law stamped on man's reason, and inwrought into the whole moral constitution of the world, reflects a divine intention beyond the simple communication of pleasure. Viewed in the light of the goal to which man is bound by all the emphasis of his moral nature, the divine aim must be considered as having included an ethical object. (3) Under a theory of creation simply for happiness, the occurrence of suffering would be inexplicable, as defeating the supreme end.

2. We will best reach the correct conclusion on this subject by observing the necessary distinction between the *subjective* and the *objective* reasons for the divine action. By the subjective reason is to be understood the divine *impulse* or motive arising from God's own nature. By the objective, the *end* at which the divine motive, as an intelligent purpose, aims. His own nature is the supreme reason of His choices and the source of His action. Because He is what He is He delights to do what He does. In acting, the relations of subject and object must be true for God Himself, unless God be really lost in a pantheistic unconsciousness which knows neither self nor ends. The subjective impulse and the objective end never exclude, but always imply and call for each other. A mother's heart is the subjective reason for her self-sacrifice, but the child's welfare is the end it seeks. Such a distinction we are not only authorized, but required to make in conceiving of the divine action. It will

help us to the true view on this question. This view must include two points:

First, the supreme reason of God's creating the universe is the subjective one, and is found in *His own goodness delighting in the exercise of the divine power and wisdom in the production of blessed existence.* Creation is a form of Love's free self-manifestation and outworking. Since God is absolutely self-sufficient, goodness is the only thing that could determine Him to the production of beings other than Himself. Personality, whether finite or infinite, is self-moving. The absolute Personality must move absolutely from Himself. In His own being was the only moving spring to the forth putting of creative energy. He created because of His fullness, self-moved in favor toward the creation He contemplated. Love is the power that takes out of self and acts non-egoistically and altruistically. Creation is altruistic activity. Guided by wisdom and holiness, love is the disposing or moving principle to God's power. The universe is an expression of the principle of communicative goodness. While it reflects God's wisdom and omnipotence, it preeminently represents His love.

Secondly, the *objective* end sought by God was the *blessedness of the creation.* This blessedness must be understood as uniting both excellence and happiness. It includes ethical as well as sensitive good. What God delights in, and therefore sought to give existence to, is not creature enjoyment alone, but real excellence of being. Since His action was altruistic, we are entitled to say that in creating the universe He sought *it,* and not Himself. It is the nature of love to communicate itself, to act for the production of excellence and happiness, to create objects on which it may pour out its favor. It would be in conflict with this law of love to make God's creative action but a movement bending back on Himself, a curve of outgoing and returning, with the supreme end of displaying His own glory. It *does* display His glory, and all the more radiantly because not an act of self-seeking, but of love. In a high sense, too, the creation is "for Himself," *i.e.,* it is for the action of His love and goodness. "For Thy pleasure they are and were created." When we thus look upon the excellence and felicity of the creation as the objective terminus of the creative action, we see the object sought in the object created, and yet leave the entire and supreme reason (*ratio*) of creation in God Himself. This answer to the whole question seems best to accord with the demands of reason, and at the same time leaves room for the great fact which Christianity brings to our view, the fact of *divine self-sacrifice*, by which, in redemption, God still seeks the welfare and happiness of His creatures. If love may be held as the supreme reason of redemption, it may certainly be of creation. The explanation throws the reasons and ends of creation and redemption into harmony.

3. As a subordinate topic under this general question, we naturally inquire into *the specific end for our own world*. We may justly say, indeed, that God sought *all* the distinct objects represented and accomplished in the existence, experiences, and true uses of all the various parts of the world's constitution and inhabitants. Myriads of different aims are everywhere and for ever passing into fulfilment and illustrating the richness of nature's teleology. But since this constitution exhibits a vast range of graded and ascending correlations, or a coordinated and advancing scheme, we necessarily ask for its ultimate and all-comprehending purpose, as one of the worlds of the great universe. We seek a teleology for the earth in its material and organic development and human history.

Clearly, if we interpret the significance of the order of subordinations and progression of existence and life on our planet, the purpose of the earth must be held as culminating in the service and destiny of man. We are aware of the scorn with which some writers have sought to cover this claim for our race, as but the pleasant self-flattery of human vanity. But, undeniably, science puts man, with his mental and moral endowments and possibilities, at the summit of nature on our globe. The inorganic parts of the earth look to the organic, the vegetable to the animal, the animal organization is crowned in the human. The human rises into the realm of free spiritual being. The movement of the grand series of advances and ascents, traced up along the slow progress of the geologic periods, shows no sign of anything higher,

"The diapason closing full in man."

To him are given attributes which place him in rulership over the whole realm of nature. Though his physical organization is embraced in it, his spiritual and rational endowments stand, in a sense, above it. In the vast rock-ages nature was prophetic of his coming, providing for his life and industries; now it submits its forces, and laws, and wealth of productions to his knowledge, will, and uses. This does not mean that each specific thing on earth exists solely for him. There are innumerable distinct and real provisions for other and subordinate ends. The order of nature is so arranged as to make each particular being reciprocally an end and a means with respect to others. But the number and proportion that terminate on human life give it this lofty preeminence. This is the crown and explanation of nature. "Man is, so far as this earth is concerned, the highest end to which nature has attained, and toward which it has always been striving. He seems to be endowed with all the forces of nature, as well as with the powers of spirit. They are all taken up and represented in him.... All this plainly indicates that man is at the head of all creatures here on the earth, and to him all nature is and always has been tributary."

It is not theology alone that asserts this view. It is preeminently the doctrine of science. Science is everywhere revealing the goal of nature's forces in the utilities of human life and welfare. Even evolution is offering its concurring word for it. "The Darwinian theory shows us distinctly, for the first time, how the creation and perfecting of man is the goal toward which nature's work has been all the while tending. It develops tenfold the significance of human life, places it upon even a loftier eminence than poets or prophets have imagined, and makes it seem more than ever the chief object of that creative activity which is manifested in the physical universe.... Not the production of any higher creature, but the perfecting of humanity, is to be the glorious consummation of nature's long and tedious work." We need not accept this evolutionary hypothesis, but in thus assigning man's place, it does homage to the invincible teleological force of the vast system of nature's indications. The highest point to which the converging lines of our world's arrangements and adaptations seem intended to look is the welfare of the human race.

4. The lofty position thus given man is justly viewed as implying something of high importance or worth in his nature. There must be in his happiness and possibilities a value that justifies, even to the divine reason, this marshalling of so many agencies and operations to his use, and consummating a world's history in his service. We must, therefore, interpret his rational and spiritual nature as being no ordinary or temporary endowment, but one which exalts him to a divine fellowship and a destined immortality. This interpretation is sustained by many and varied lines of confirmatory evidence. In all ages and nations the race has developed and cherished belief in a continued existence after death. Literature, from the time of Plato down to the present, has busied itself with this hope and its reasons. Man has everywhere interpreted his destiny as higher than that of the grass that withers and the beasts that perish. In his aspirations after ideals never reached in this life, in a sense of constitutional possibilities and adaptations in his being not fulfilled here, he has read his appointment to a larger and higher field of thought and action in some future sphere. These common "intimations of immortality" have not been discredited, but have been vindicated and assured by the best and latest science and philosophy. The human soul, with the great attributes of reason, freedom, and ethical responsibility, is irresolvable in any combination, interaction, or motion of matter. No chemistry of the material elements or processes of molecular action can explain the origination of thought and personality. "By no possibility can thought and feeling be in any sense the products of matter." Self-determination and memory refuse all physical solution. "It is absolutely and forever inconceivable that a number of carbon, hydrogen, nitrogen, and oxygen atoms should be otherwise than indifferent to their positions and motions, past, present, or future. It is utterly inconceivable how consciousness should result from their joint action." Man, therefore, as a personal being, is spirit and hyper-material. His high attributes lift him into communion with his Creator, and place him above the destiny of merely physical organization. The endowments and provisions of his

soul are prophetic, and pledge much that is unrealized in the present life. Kant's great theistic argument, it will be remembered, finds sufficient evidence, not only of the existence of a righteous God, but of a future state, in the intrinsic constitution of the soul, which shows that it has been made for a happiness and a moral excellence unattainable in this world. The proof of both God and immortality is found in the laws of man's being. The grand fact of personality, in all that the fact involves as to man's essence and powers, makes him in a high sense a child of the infinite Father of spirits, and justifies not only the old poet's exultant claim:

"We are also His offspring,"

but the common human faith which disdains "the lot of the grass that withers and the beasts that perish," and counts on living forever. And thus Natural Theology, by the processes through which it has reached the evidences of the existence of an infinite Author of the universe, obtains at the same time a new and higher conception of the relationship and destiny of the human race. In finding God it also finds man.

In here closing this outline view of the great subject presented, it is proper to add the confession of Natural Theology, that it cannot open up all the truth needed by man's religious nature or required by the moral and spiritual interests of the race. It does, indeed, assure and vindicate the great fundamental truth of the existence of God, and throw explaining light on numberless facts of nature and life and problems of thought and duty. The truths which it vindicates are of incalculable moment. But beyond all that we can learn concerning God and His relation to the world from reason and nature, there is room and necessity for the light and teaching of a supernatural revelation.

1. Natural Theology can give only a partial and incomplete view of God's character.
2. It leaves us in the dark as to man's specific end in life and how he may accomplish it.
3. Its intimations, though they suggest hope for the future, yet fail to bring immortality to full light.

4. It does not explain the existence of sin and the depravity of our race.

5. It furnishes no remedy for sin—no way of forgiveness, or salvation from it.

6. The history of mankind shows unquestionably that when left to the mere light of nature and reason men hold low and inadequate conceptions of God, and are woefully wanting in the knowledge necessary to a right, pure, and happy life. Even the most cultured nations, without God's word, have failed to attain a clear or steady conception of his character and will.

7. A revelation from God gives a fresh and most impressive proof of His existence. As we have His revelation of Himself in the Holy Scriptures of the Old and New Testaments, His character and will are fully made known. The great questions of truth and duty are answered. In God's light we see light.

www.ingramcontent.com/pod-product-compliance
Lightning Source LLC
LaVergne TN
LVHW051115080426
835510LV00018B/2056